The Gods Sleep Through It All

A collection of essays

Wonder Guchu

Mwanaka Media and Publishing Pvt Ltd,
Chitungwiza Zimbabwe
*
Creativity, Wisdom and Beauty

Publisher:

Mmap

Mwanaka Media and Publishing Pvt Ltd

24 Svosve Road, Zengeza 1

Chitungwiza Zimbabwe

mwanaka@yahoo.com

https//mwanakamediaandpublishing.weebly.com

Distributed in and outside N. America by African Books Collective

orders@africanbookscollective.com

www.africanbookscollective.com

ISBN: 978-1-77906-358-8

EAN: 9781779063588

DISCLAIMER

All views expressed in this publication are those of the author and do not necessarily reflect the views of Mmap.

Dedication

For all those whose lives were eaten by misgovernance,
corruption, leadership idiocy and those whose lives
will be eaten by the same in the next 1 000 years

*****

Books by the same author

Sketches of High Density Life (2004)
My Children, My Home (2007)
Kumafulatsi (2016)
Threshold of Time (poetry collection, (2018)
Taimbove Nenyika (poetry collection, (2018)

Acroynms

ANC	African National Congress
AU	African Union
ARVs	Anti-retroviral drugs
BAT	British American Tobacco
BP	British Petrol
CEPR	Centre for Economic and Policy Research
CIA	Central Intelligence Agency
CoD	Congress of Democrats
Cope	Congress of the People
ECLAC	United Nations Economic Commission for Latin America and the Caribbean
ESAP	Economic Structural Adjustment Programme
FBI	Federal Bureau of Investigations
GMO	Genetically Modified Organism
IMF	International Monetary Fund
JCTR	Justice Centre for Theological Reflection
LIC	Low-intensity conflict
MDC	Movement for Democratic Change
MDC-T	Movement for Democratic Change – Tsvangirai
NECF	National Economic Consultative Forum
RBZ	Reserve Bank of Zimbabwe
RDP	Rally for Democracy and Progress
SADC	Southern African Development Community
SAP	Structural Adjustment Programme
SAPRIN	Structural Adjustment Participatory Review International Network
Tazama	Tanzania Zambia Malawi

Tazara	Tanzania Zambia Railways
UNDP	United Nations Development Programme
Unip	United National Independent Party
Zanu-PF	Zimbabwe National Union-Patriotic Front
Zidera Act	Zimbabwe Democracy and Economic Recovery Act
Zimpapers	Zimbabwe Newspaper (1980)
Zimprest Transformation	Zimbabwe Programme for Economic and Social Transformation
ZOU	Zimbabwe Open University

Table of Contents

Introduction

There are very few success stories in as far as governance in Africa is concerned decades after the first African country Ghana gained independence in 1957. Since then most of the newly formed governments were destabilised by western sponsored coups - that is in the early years when the former colonisers were directly involved such as in the case of Patrice Lumumba of the Congo who was murdered in 1960.

In the latter years, African leaders have mastered the art of destabilising their own countries by stealing state resources; overstaying their welcome; killing their rivals and rigging elections.

Most of them still blame the colonisers for the state of their countries, yet they choose to forget their hand in it.

Africa is still backward in this age as if we are under colonisation. Very few countries have functioning governments that deliver services and work for the people. Even educated leaders have not been of much help to their people. Today, sad to say, the situation in some African countries is worse than it was during colonialism.

Look at the exodus of the youth who are seeking better lives in Europe or the US. They do not feel at home in Africa to the extent of sacrificing their lives daring the high seas. Look at the mushrooming squatter camps in every town where the people live like animals. One would argue that the colonialists limited the number of individuals who come to work and stay in cities, but equally so, one might also argue that there is no need for a few people to own large pieces of land in the towns. One might argue that it is unjustified for a few to own 60 houses in the same city when millions have no decent shelter.

The same can be said about services in hospitals and schools where infrastructure is either decaying or non-existent. The poor and disadvantaged suffer while the leaders fly around the world to seek treatment. Even their children attend schools outside the country while those from impoverished families have to make do with scantily resourced schools. What about the people who do not have government support?

Africa's problem is leadership and not the former colonisers.

As Africans, we can help matters by speaking truth to power. Indeed, when one does that there are consequences but then if you cannot demonstrate on the streets, then write about it or sing about it. It does not matter if we now have black leaders, we should call them to order. Bob Marley once said:

If you're white and you're wrong, then you're wrong; if you're black and you're wrong, you're wrong. People are people. Black, blue, pink, green - God make no rules about colour; only society makes rules where my people suffer, and that's why we must have redemption and redemption now.

Some of these essays date back to 2012 when I was a columnist for the regional *Southern Times* newspaper. Although this is a project jointly run by the governments of Namibia and Zimbabwe, I was a bit careful with the way I put across my ideas. The majority of the essays appeared in *The Namibian* newspaper. You will find that in these essays, I did not hold back. I have also included a few notes to a number of essays to give background.

Windhoek, February 2018

It's Lonely Dying in Africa

In November 2015 Paris experienced a series of terrorist attacks that left more than 130 people dead and several hundred others injured. At about the same time, Boko Haram carried out attacks in Nigeria leaving hundred dead and several other hundred dead. All the other deaths did not raise the world's eyebrows. In the case of the Paris attacks, world leaders went to France in a show of solidarity yet none has done that for Nigeria.

The picture of European leaders marching with arms locked in Paris on 11 January 2015 in a show of unity, solidarity and defiance against terrorism brought one sad reality to us: We never unite for anything good in Africa!

And the more than four million people who converged for the solidarity march in French cities after the killing of 17 people by suspected terrorists last week also drove home the point that our brotherhood in Africa is just lip-service. It makes us appear heartless because during the same period, Boko Haram also massacred hundreds in Nigeria and nobody on the continent did anything in solidarity.

What happened to our humanity? Our sense of unity? The African traits that drove Kenneth Kaunda, Jomo Kenyatta and Julius Nyerere to sacrifice their countries and resources for the freedom of others on the continent? What happened to home-grown ubuntu and Ujamaa and Harambee with a human face? Those national ideologies which enabled Africans in Zambia, Tanzania and Kenya to open up their countries and hearts to help others seeking help to gain independence?

When the attacks started in France last week, every cable news network in Europe and America suspended their programming to focus on the event. We were taken, in movie style, through the police efforts as they chased the suspects until the last minute they were shot dead.

And days after the shooting, cable news networks too followed up the story and made sure those in power are moved to act.

In contrast, the hundreds in Nigeria died alone. The story of their needless deaths also received lukewarm media coverage in Africa. It was third after the Air Asia tragedy and the French attacks internationally.

This was reminiscent of the more than 800 000 Tutsis who were massacred in 1994 while Africa pretended not to see or hear anything. They too died lonely deaths. They died while Africa waited for Europe and America to act and speak against the massacres. Even the 7 000 plus who succumbed to the Ebola virus died lonely deaths. The same with mothers and children who die needless deaths on the continent because of lack of proper medical care. They die while we are waiting for Europe to pump in money. Or send personnel in the form of Doctors Without Borders to help our people out of misery.

So this is Africa. The rising continent? The selfish continent. The heartless continent. The only continent where, most probably, we have leaders who are vocal over trifles. Leaders who hide when they are needed the most.

Here we wait for Europe to speak for us. We forget that Europe speaks for herself. For her children. And that Africa must and should speak for herself. And for her children.

Europe has done enough fighting and talking for us. Wherever there is a war on the continent, Africa has looked up to Europe for help with peacekeeping. Or negotiations. Wherever there has been a disease outbreak on the continent, Africa has looked up to Europe for help in finding a cure. Or containment. It was Europe that came up with massive support for fighting HIV in Africa. European presidents ran schemes to help orphans and provide information on how to deal with the disease. All that we heard from our leaders were speeches and a few first ladies hogging the limelight from running HIV-Aids schemes that relied on funding from Europe or America.

The ongoing Ebola virus outbreak would have wiped out large communities in some African countries had it not been for Europe. Still today, there are European teams on the continent containing the Ebola virus.

Even in demanding our freedoms, we have given it to Europe. Imagine, asking Europe to help us remove from power the leaders we would have elected! The dictators we would have created. How lame have we become?

As for Nigeria, more than 200 schoolgirls* abducted by Boko Haram in May last year are still missing. Time is slowly but surely burying them while Africa waits for Europe or America to lead the search to find her daughters.

And we still want to tell ourselves that we are independent. That we are free when we cannot help ourselves? Defend our people? Provide for ourselves? And above all ask Europe or America to stand back while we sort out our issues as Africans?

Just count how many European forces are trying to stop us from killing each other in Africa. Check how many have been deployed to help us improve ourselves. Look at the number of doctors from Europe, America or some other outpost across the world. Yes, the African Union (AU) has a peacekeeping force in Somalia but one that is being funded by Europe and America. Even the AU headquarters in Addis Ababa is a US$200 million gift from China.

Africa's fathers look to other men to build their homes for them and still walk tall and tell their children that they are real parents.

Where is Africa? Where is the AU? Do we need the AU? What is the use for leaders to waste resources flying to Addis Ababa for talks when nothing comes out of these?

It is time Africa stopped being a talking head and become a busy body in solving problems bedevilling her children. Europe does. America does. China does. Why not Africa? We are good at complaining and grumbling and demanding. Most of the times, we accuse and blame Europe for interfering with our business in Africa, yet we forget that we allow that situation. We take a back seat when we should be leading in solving our problems.

- 13 January 2015

---

* *On the night of 14–15 April 2014, 276 girls were kidnapped from Chibok Government Secondary School in the town of Chibok in Borno State, Nigeria. Boko Haram claimed responsibility for the kidnappings. About 57 of the schoolgirls managed to escape a few months later, while more were released in a prisoner exchange deal.*

Death by a Thousand Cuts

Corruption is like a thread that links countries on the African continent. I have experienced it first-hand in the three countries cited in this column. Shocking to me was Botswana where the government declared a zero-tolerance on corruption yet the bug has over the years burrowed into civil servants' hearts. It is like witnessing an illness slowly consuming your beloved child. And you stand there, hurt and hopeless because you cannot do anything. Something dies in you as the disease grows.

I have travelled Botswana for about ten years now. A clean country. A lawful citizenry. And a police force bent on upholding the rule of law. An immigration that works without looking at faces. For six years, this clean image of Botswana sat on my mind.

Four years ago, I was stopped between Gaborone and Francistown. It was a 60 kilometres per hour stretch, and I was doing about 100 kilometres an hour. I was slapped with a 700 pula spot fine. I had no cash on me.

They took my passport and driver's licence and ordered me to bring the money.

Francistown was about 50 kilometres away. I rushed and returned. One of the officers took the money, peeled off five 100s, handed back my documents, and waved me away.

My eyes watered, weeping the slow death Africa dies every day.

Last year, Christmas time. The queue at the Botswana border post was thick, long, immobile and suffocating. I braced for a long wait.

A soldier walked up to the tail end of the queue; spoke to some guys behind me. He then led them to the head of the queue. I followed. In the corner of the empty building, the officer asked each of us to pay 50 pula. He then gave us forms to complete before proceeding.

On my way back to Windhoek, my front number plate had fallen off. I had paid for it three times between Harare and Bulawayo. On the Botswana border side, a soldier stopped me. I told him I had paid for the licence plate. But he said either I parked the car at the police station or pay. I stared at him. And he said that is how it was. I then said Botswana has changed. He replied: Nothing remains the same. That his salary was not enough. That if I chose to park the car at the station, there would be more officers to pay.

How much? I asked him. How much did you pay in Zimbabwe? he asked.

US$10, I told him. Then he said: Give us US$10 each. I protested, and he said: Well, provide us with the US$10. I grudgingly did.

Mozambique, 12 years ago. I took a trip to Maputo from Harare. I was part of a group in a minibus. It was around 22h00, and we were within the city. Our driver was asleep, and I had taken over. The roadblock was around a bend, and the officer appeared from the dark. I managed to slam the brakes, and the minibus almost rolled over. He came over, asked for my licence, checked it and then told me to get off. I followed him. When we got to the makeshift table where his colleague was, the officer said I almost ran him over. Then questions rained. Their verdict: We will lock you up!

My colleagues also came over. I had been ordered to sit on the ground. One colleague understood Portuguese. After what sounded like an argument, an officer dragged him into the darkness. On return, I was 'released'. Later the colleague said he had paid.

I have run countless battles with Zimbabwean traffic police. Each time I insisted on getting a ticket and paying. Each time, I was charged more.

In 2012, 75 kilometres from Harare. I stopped at an accident scene to take pictures. An officer approached me.

I was not supposed to take pictures, he said.

Why I asked.

It is close to a roadblock, he said.

So what? I went on.

It is a security zone, he informed me.

He grabbed my camera and dragged me to the roadblock – just 20 metres away. The grilling started. These are journalists who write negatively about the country, one officer said. Which paper do you write for? Where is your accreditation? The questions came. Then demands my ID and licence. I kept quiet. For about an hour, I sat in the sun.

Then an elderly officer walked over. I see, he started, you are angry.

I kept quiet.

He went on: Look, these "kids" do not care. They will detain you. You will lose precious time.

I looked past him in disgust.

He pressed on: If you deal with me, I will sort it out.

I looked at him, my eyes watering, weeping another slow death Africa dies every day.

A mini bus driver was hauled in. He did not waste time buying his way past.

See, the elderly officer said, those are real men. Their hands don't shake.

I demanded to see the commander. The station was close by. I drove there with four officers. Fortunately, the commander knew me. He dismissed the officers, telling them I was a journalist. I asked him why such rot was being allowed openly.

His words: What can they do? They have families. In any case, some of you promote it. You offer to pay, and this is what we get.

Namibia. Last December. I had received a letter confirming my permit from home affairs and immigration late. When I inquired in Windhoek, a woman at the counter told me I could travel and show the letter at the port of entry.

When I presented the letter and my passport at Buitepos, the officer looked at me, paged through my passport and returned the documents. Go back and have the permit stamped, he said. I tried to explain, but he stood his ground. Another took my passport and checked on the computer.

You entered Namibia on an emergency travel document in April, she said, and I laughed at her because it was a lie.

They kept me for an hour. Later I told them to let me go and deny me entry on my way back. One of them said: What kind of a Zimbabwean are you?

My eyes watered, weeping yet another slow death some parts of Africa die every day.

15 July 2014

When Is Our Evolution Coming?

If there is one thing the leadership on the African continent has failed to do is to work for the good of the people. While there has been a lot of talk about how to work together, nothing ever came to fruition. The African Union cannot put together a continental army. We still expect much from the former colonisers. In simple terms, our leaders still make us behave like slaves because after failing to make the continent work, they grow hopes on loans and grants from the former colonisers. We have been unable to chart a new path and still seek help. This is why no African leader has the guts to summon former colonisers and lay down the rules of engagement. Sadly enough, the former colonisers are still dictating terms of reference and engagement even when their countries depend so much on Africa.

So they ran. In dozens. Falling over themselves. Spending millions on fuel. And travel allowances. Our esteemed presidents. Just like they always run. China-Africa summit. France-Africa summit. Africa-EU summit. Now the US-Africa summit. They plead for help. Beg for investment. Cry about African diseases. Poverty. Stunted development. Unemployment. Sit in long meetings. Deliberate about Africa. But still, return to dying cities. Rising unemployment statistics. Rising mortality rates. Reduced life spans.

They pledge African resources. Animals. Jobs. Land. Everything as long as the summit hosts pledge a little money to create a few jobs. This is how small we are. Pliable. Shortsighted. Generous to a fault.

Just when are we going to be our investors? If we have the resources, what is it that we do not have? When is the African evolution coming? Who should beg? Us with our loads of valuable resources? Who should call the shots? The seller or the buyer?

Our leaders beat their chest. Africa is the richest. A gem of a continent. We beg to sell off all these to the highest bidder. It is an investment. Africa needs investors, they say. And when they run to the West, they pose for pictures. Them and their women. Put on grey smiles. After that then shopping sprees. Back home nothing changes. Under the tree, classes go on. Empty, decaying hospitals open their doors. Weary and hungry villagers stream in to spend the day waiting for the only nurse. To while away the time waiting for God's call.

The jobless wake-up. To stand by the roadside. Or to walk the same path to a job centre. For another wait. Long hopeless wait. Their job is to look for a job. They age. They resign. They retire. Still jobless.

Right now, somewhere on the continent, some bodies lie abandoned in the streets. Ravaged by Ebola. Nobody wants them. Nobody wants death. Whole villages closed off. Towns blanketed. Death stalks the continent. Somewhere just outside the city, the lucky ones lie in shallow graves. Hastily dug. Quickly buried. Nobody goes there. Thrown away.

Cities stir up. Tired smoke from weak industries struggles to reach the skies. Rickety jalopies rattle along the potholed roads. Negotiating paths through another long day. Laden with hopeful and ever smiling faces. Domestic workers. Labourers. Government clerks. Nurses. Teachers. Waiting for a better day. A pleasant time. For evolution.

They have seen revolutions. Participated. Lost loved ones. Everything too. Souls included. And they hoped with the end of the revolution; they will find hope. Chart a new path. Be people unto themselves. Live off the resources in their country. And never beg again for a chance to live. To reproduce. To die dignified deaths.

They wait for evolution. But African evolution is a mirage. Fleeting shadows. A rainbow. Beautiful. Unreachable. Same as our resources. So near, yet so far.

China-Africa summit. France-Africa summit. EU-Africa summit. And now US-Africa summit. The summit hosts will run to Africa. Open up mines. Bring in their experts. Rope in a few of us. For wheelbarrows. Picks and shovels. After all, we do not need much. Our lives are simple. We need no cars of our own. No decent houses of our own. We must just make do.

So they take our gold. Uranium. Diamonds. Open banks to siphon our money off. Develop their cities with our wealth. Cart our resources for their factories. Create jobs for their people. Then open shops in our towns to sell products made in Europe from our resources. And we pay hard.

We wait for evolution to come. That day when we can have President Hifikepunye Pohamba* calling for a Namibia-Europe summit. That day when President Goodluck Jonathan* will host a Nigeria-China summit. That day when President Jacob Zuma can hold a South Africa-France summit. We wait for those days when our leaders can call the shots. The day when we become our investors. The day when we realise that it is not true that we do not have the resources. Money even. Experts too. It is not true that Africa cannot do it for herself. How can we not be able to invest in our economies when we have been independent for 50 years? Why do we still look outside? Run every time we are summoned. Crawl when we get a chance to appear before other leaders. Beg for them to come and take away our resources.

When is our evolution coming? And why does it seem as if we are evolving backwards? While they are rushing to summits, our youth unemployment rises.

- 19 August 2014

*Hifikepunye Pohamba was Namibia's President from 2005 until 2015.

* Goodluck Jonathan was Nigerian President from 2010-2015.

* Robert Mugabe was Zimbabwe's leader from 1980-2017

* Jacob Zuma was South Africa's president from 2008-2018

Who Needs Education to Ruin a Country?

Towards the Swapo Party elective congress in 2012, there was talk about some candidates being uneducated enough to be in leadership positions. Swapo's elective congress is decisive because the party has what is called a pot. This is a list of people who will qualify for parliament or be chosen as ministers or deputy ministers. There was much talk about education regarding those whose names were in the pot. It set me thinking whether education is all that it takes for a person to be a good leader. Various examples of so-called educated African leaders have shown that education is not everything to being a great leader.

There is talk about a lack of experience for some of Swapo's chosen 'pot' candidates. Honestly now, who needs the experience to destroy a country? What education is required to mess up? History is full of very educated people who, as leaders, ruined their countries. A sign that experience and education have nothing to do with politics.

This is why nobody is required to apply for a ministerial job. Or for the state presidency. There are no interviews or a merit-based selection process.

In most cases all one is required to do is outdo the other person vying for the same post. It does not matter how the race is run. Intimidation. Character assassinations. Threadbare lies. Underhand dealings. Promises for jobs to sycophants. Anything as long as the contest is won.

If there were interviews done, would Jacob Zuma of South Africa have passed such an interview? As for what? To do what? We all know how Julius Malema pushed for Zuma's ascendancy. Maybe and most probably, Michael Sata* of Zambia would also not have made it. Maybe, just maybe, President Hifikepunye Pohamba* would also never have made it. Even Joseph Kabila of the DRC would not be there. All of them. But they did. And are. And maybe, just maybe, Robert Mugabe of Zimbabwe with his bagful of degrees would have made it. But again look at what he has done to the country and his people. Millions have left to find sources of survival elsewhere.

This is why talking about experience in politics is like looking for virgins among sex workers. You will not find any because politicians and sex workers have one thing in common – hard-doing everything in sight. It does not matter how they do it, as long it is done. And both do it very well such that when they are done, anything left intact is fortunate.

This is what Mugabe – with his bagful of degrees – and a cabinet full of experienced politicians have done to Zimbabwe. Once the African jewel. A virgin at independence in 1980. An inspiration to many. An education system that sits atop continental lists. An example of reconciliation. President Robert Mugabe. Very well-educated. A bag full of degrees. Articulate. Thirty-four years' experience as a leader. A teacher. A guerrilla leader. A prime minister. A president. Attended several conferences over 35 years. Gained more certificates of attendance. And honorary ones too.

The politicians. Thirty years or more of experience. Most of them. Shuffled from one ministry to the other. Jacks of all trades. And incompetent to the hilt. Making laws. Amending some. Repealing others. Even laws they had no idea of.

Zimbabweans. Very educated. Sought after experts. Undoubting performers. An unfaltering determination. People who refuse to go

14

down with the economy. Smiling even when the pain bites deeper. Limping along on one leg. Eyes set on tomorrow. Most are polite. But we have been shat on big time by our well-educated and experienced leaders.

If indeed experience matters, Mugabe would be the best leader in the world. For leaders are measured by what they do and do not do for their people. Zimbabwe could be the most developed country on the continent. Zimbabweans, the happiest people in the world. The Zimbabwean economy, bursting at the seams with surplus money and goods.

But nay, with all his education and experience, Mugabe gropes. Stumbles. Blames. Accuses. Thinks he is right. Always. That there are forces against him. That he will prevail. He is unaware of the sinkhole he has dug for the country and his people. Mugabe blames sanctions and not corruption. He accuses the West, not himself and his lot that loot at will. They plunder as if there is no tomorrow.

With all their experience, Mugabe's ministers sit oblivious of the decay enveloping them. They sleep in their graduation gowns while half the population has fled. They are unaware that the industries have gone dead quiet. That the country is on death row.

Today, most of Mugabe's children are refugees across the globe. Even in Iceland. Fleeing a ruined country. A mauled economy. A country runs on borrowed currency used to buy imported commodities. Aye, we Mugabe's people, educated as we are, scattered all over the world, wonder what happened. Wandering, lost in time and events. Seeking relevance. An assurance that somewhere humanity still exists. Disbelieving that such experienced and well-educated leaders can ruin such a beautiful country.

Aye, we Mugabe's people, experienced as we are, could not do anything to stop the educated and experienced politicians from messing up the country. Eating up the economy. Hard doing us. Aye, for all that has gone on. Going on. Will go on. Zimbabweans will still vote for the same people. Even when it is clear that of the 2,2 million jobs promised in 2013, not a single one has been created.

The same old men and women will still be there – using their wrong experience to destroy the country. And the educated ones will still be running to vote and defend them.

So never fool yourself, politics has never been about experience and education. It is purely a dumb business.

- *9 September 2014*

Michael Sata died in October 2014 while Hifikepunye Pohamba retired in 2014 after serving two-terms

Too Many Opposition Parties But No Politicians

Election time in almost every African country brings about all sorts of people claiming to be politicians. They make promises and turn up dust on the campaign trail, but when they lose, they disappear as fast as they would have come into the woodworks. In Zimbabwe, for example, such people or political parties have been called special projects either for the ruling party Zanu-PF or some other interested party meant to split the vote. Whether the part of splitting the votes is true or not is another issue at this moment because what matters is the fact that most African countries at election time experiences so many opposition parties but none or those leading the parties are politicians. This is democracy but how much does it create opportunities for the ruling parties at the expense of the opposition that would need every vote to win?

Not everyone who forms an opposition party is a politician. Most of these people do not have the pull factor, and they cannot even lie to move a mountain. No wonder in Africa, mostly, one finds a president for life and a party ruling for eternity. The reason why some countries wait for half a century to vote for change.

It is mostly in Africa where one also finds opposition parties by the thousands and aspiring presidents by six dozens but still the electorate does not see anything worth their while in them.

Most opposition parties look at the ruling parties's failures for reasons to convince the electorate. They do not introspect and ask themselves if they are worth a politician's salt.

Most ruling parties in Africa have honed their lies to perfection such that they have been telling the same lies with conviction for decades. They are not ashamed of it. They can look into the cameras and repeat the same fibs with straight faces ... the same fibs for a hundred years if need be. And still, the electorate votes for them without batting an eyelid. Still, the electorate gushes and laps up the lies with smiles. That is politicking.

But what do we get from most if not all opposition parties – blunt calls for the ruling party to just leave power! Who does that? Giving over power in Africa just like that? Without a fight? Much of what we get from opposition parties are reactions against messing up by ruling parties. Condemnation and vilifications. They waste most of their time discussing the ruling parties without addressing the electorates' concerns.

The electorate is very much aware of the transgressions the ruling parties commit against them. They want change. They look for something better. But the opposition does nothing but chorus the ruling parties' abuse of the people.

This could explain why across Africa, there are times when an opposition party emerges. It stirs the people's imagination. Drives them to the voting booth. For once, people see hope. They believe in tomorrow. Such parties will manage to grab more than ten parliamentary seats.

This was the case with Congress of the People (Cope) in South Africa. That was also the same with the Movement for Democratic Change (MDC) in Zimbabwe. Namibia has the Rally for Democracy and Progress (RDP). Before the RDP, there was the Congress of Democrats (CoD). A few years down the line, people's hopes die when they realise that while there is an opposition party, there are no politicians. That voting for such leaders is akin to groping in the dark for a lost needle.

When such parties emerge, they benefit from the protest votes from an angry electorate seeking change. They get grudge votes from those who have lost trust with and in the ruling parties. Then they rest on their laurels. Almost every opposition party that benefited from this anger and lack of trust however squandered the chances. They strangled the people's hopes. When the next election comes, there will be no protest or grudge votes because the people would have given up on the opposition. If there are any protest votes, they will be directed at the inept opposition instead.

Indeed, Cope did exactly that. Soon after the small victory, the leaders started fighting each other over money and positions. Years were spent fighting individual wars while the electorate's desires were thrown into the dustbin. The court case took long and drained the leaders of all the energy that could have been exerted towards effecting change for the common man and woman. Today, Cope is nothing but a grouping of old people waiting to die as opposition members.

The same happened with and to MDC. In the less than 20 years the party has been in existence, it has been hit by three major splits. The party squandered all the time and energy on internal fights while Zanu-PF was ruling the roost. The party also targeted fertile brains and purged them out, leaving dumb-heads. Today, what is left of MDC is nothing but squandered chances, regrets, wishes and a slow death.

The RDP did not suffer any splits but was shaken terribly. The recent landslide victories scored by Swapo in the few by-elections are enough to point at a wasted RDP that will never mount any meaningful challenge to Swapo. It is foolhardy for anybody to dream of getting more seats than they got in the last election because the electorate, like abused women, is trapped in a relationship with Swapo.

The conclusion is very simple: the African National Congress will rule forever. Imagine with Jacob Zuma's shenanigans; his party still managed to romp past all the opposition parties. It means Zanu-PF will also be there for as long as the grieving and the poverty-stricken Zimbabweans wish. Even today when Zanu-PF is at its weakest with fights over who should succeed Robert Mugabe, the opposition is nowhere to be seen. They are busy aiming cheap shots at each other.

In Kenya Daniel Arap Moi always beat the opposition although the votes cast for his party were always fewer than those of the splintered opposition put together. It also means that Swapo shall rule even when 30 other opposition parties are formed. This is as certain as the fact that there are too many opposition parties, but no politicians.

This will prevail until the opposition parties realise that they should, at least, talk about what the people want to hear. Focusing on the wrongs done by the ruling parties is not an answer to what the opposition will do if given the protest vote.

- 11 November 2014

Europe and Migrants – The Game Has Changed

Europe's situation with the flood of refugees from Syria and elsewhere is akin to the bird snatching the catapult from the hunter. In simple terms, this means the game has changed! Indeed, for Europe and Britain, the migrants are a reminder of their shameful deeds in foreign lands where they gladly pour in money just to disrupt lives and lay to waste the future of generations.

As it is now, bah the reasons for Europe's involvement in Syria, Libya, Iraq, and many other countries in Africa, the problems they created for the inhabitants of those countries are following them home. Once Europe, Britain and America would travel distances to cause havoc and death and hopelessness and leave burning countries in their wake. Those used to cause the mayhem will go back to sleep peacefully and live comfortably looking after their cute children while the inhabitants of the lands they would have laid to waste are being killed, maimed, tortured, brutalised and wasted.

This happened to Africa in the early years of independence.

The Stockholm-based International Peace Research Institute says there were 60 successful coups in Africa between 1956 and 1985 – an average of two coups per year. To show how Europe was scared, 1968 saw a spike in coups with 64 failed and several successful ones. Writing in Governance, Security and Conflict

Resolution in Africa, researcher Anyang' Nyong'o, says 50 African states were under military rule by 1986.

In Togo, for example, the first elected African leader, Sylvanus Olympio, was seen as a threat for his grassroots approach to issues when his country gained independence in 1961 from the French. Two years later, Olympio was overthrown and assassinated in what is most probably the first bloody coup on the African continent.

After the sponsored coup that saw Patrice Lumumba assassinated, more than three million Congolese have been killed in long running wars. In all these coups, Europe, Britain and the US never felt the pain of their actions because they happened far away.

Lately, the same Europe, Britain and the US have been ganging up to cause further social unrest by funding groups to destroy, kill and maim. Without defending dictatorships, the methods used by Europe, Britain and the US have not brought any change but worsened the situation.

There has not been any liberation for the Libyans from Gadaffi. The Iraqis are living in fear. Syria has seen four years of war and billions of dollars from Europe, Britain and the US to fund death. Indeed, people must be freed from dictators but what freedom is it that we see in Libya, Syria, Iraq and Afghanistan? Why should Europe, Britain and the US run away after killing targeted dictators and without any plan for making sure that there would be peace after their unsolicited intervention?

But the game, like Franz Fanon, would say, has changed comrades. Europe will not find sleep because the problems they create elsewhere are following them home.

Syrians want jobs, houses and a country to call their own and raise their children. So they follow the ruinous money trail to Europe.

But Europe is not happy with their work. Listen to them blaming each other. Hungary says it's Germany's problem. Yes, these Christians are not pretending anymore to love and to care and to accommodate. The Christian mask they wear when they want to control weaker and rich-but-poor countries has fallen off.

It is clear that it is cheap talk meant to lull and calm those whose resources Europe plunder. Those whose lands Europe grab. And those whose future they steal. Europe has never been an all-weather friend. Sadly, weakened nations never learn. Here is Fanon:

Come, then, comrades; it would be as well to decide at once to change our ways. We must shake off the heavy darkness in which we were plunged, and leave it behind. The new day which is already at hand must find us firm, prudent and resolute. We must leave our dreams and abandon our old beliefs and friendships of the time before life began. Let us waste no time in sterile litanies and nauseating mimicry. Leave this Europe where they are never done talking of man; yet murder men everywhere they find them, at the corner of every one of their streets, in all the corners of the globe. For centuries they have stifled almost the whole of humanity in the name of a so-called spiritual experience. Look at them today swaying between atomic and spiritual disintegration.

Yes, comrades, the game has changed; the bird now has the catapult so the hunter must be scared.
- *8 September 2015*

A Continent of Little Scruples

J ust wondering. How does it work? Most governments - African governments to be precise - spend more than half of their budgets on non-essentials.

Presidential jets and imported high-powered luxury cars - at least three for each minister. A Mercedes-Benz for cruising city roads, a 4x4 for the neglected rural roads and another for picking up children from school. Again, just wondering. What is more sensible, easier and cheaper? Using millions of dollars to repair the neglected roads that wear down the cars or spending millions buying cars that will be worn down by the neglected roads?

More resources are devoted to bloated ministries. Resources are spent on the minister, his deputy who cannot act when the minister is away and cannot even attend Cabinet meetings. More resources are spent on a permanent secretary, a deputy permanent secretary, an undersecretary and a host of directors and their deputies. Just wondering. If a deputy minister (in most cases and many African countries) cannot act in the absence of a minister, what is their job? Are deputies not supposed to be in charge if their bosses are away?

Most public services in Africa remain cold. Unmonitored. Insensitive. Indifferent. Incoherent. Nobody seems to know who is doing or not doing what. In this maze of confusion, the State bleeds. Nothing much is left for skills training and well-equipped and better-staffed schools. For happy, well-fed teachers. Nothing is left for village clinics. No medicine, no nurses, no ambulances.

And for this shortfall, African governments will beg the Chinese for development funds for roads, bridges, storage tanks and job creation. Of course, the Chinese will build roads, bridges and storage tanks. But these roads do not lead to the nearest clinic or school - for the Chinese do not care about schools. Hence no China schools or China clinics and no China hospitals. They will build roads leading to the nearest Chinatown. For they know where the money is. The market for their cheap goods. Containerised shipments from their homeland. Most of it smuggled and counterfeit even. Abibas. Not Adidas. Halvin Ylein. Not Calvin Klein. Niek. Not Nike. Guggi. Not Gucci.

Even the money goes out the way the goods come in. Externalised, smuggled out from millions of small Chinese shops scattered all over the continent. The money is untaxed and unaccounted for. Just lots of money being syphoned from the continent. Of course, there are jobs created - but for the modern day slave who gets starvation wages, no benefits and no respect.

The Chinese master can even defecate in a plastic shopping bag and ask the desperate African labourer to cart away the stinky parcel. No recourse. No complaints. All this on the motherland.

Yes, they will build roads but those that lead to a Chinese-owned mine. The nearest oil field. Or the land they own. They create more jobs but mostly for their poor kinsfolk. Those rescued from the jaws of grinding poverty in deep rural, remote China. Ordinary guys passed as experts. Bricklayers, carpenters, cleaners and drivers. Useless and even unemployable people in China turn experts overnight once on African soil and take up exported jobs.

And some leaders complain. They have criticised, castigated and threatened. But their voices die amid promises of low-interest loans. Next, we hear how China is an all-weather friend, coming a long way from the years of the struggle.

African governments also beg the US and the West for medicines, ARVs, mosquito nets, circumcision clippers, monetary donations, expertise, textbooks, schools and bursaries. And the US and the West will give all these, send their people as volunteer corps, create bonds, establish forums and call for conferences.

The US-Africa Infrastructure Conference, US-Africa Business Forum, UK-Africa Investment Forum, US and the UK this and that come to mind, with Africa coming second - always. And our African leaders smile broadly and carelessly. But the US and the UK will set conditions. Their enemies become your enemy. If they sanction Iran, then you too must sanction Iran. If they fight anyone, that too must be your fight. Never bite the hand that feeds you. Lest the food is taken away. Whenever the 'gifts' come, the whole country is supposed to stand still. Eyes lifted upwards in gratitude. Arms clasped in reverence. What's the choice? A mortgaged people.

And our African leaders make grand entries. Sleek. Gliding in black limousines. Hiding behind darkened windows. Sirens wailing to announce their arrival. Fake smiles and gratitude. Just to inaugurate a road donated by China. To receive books bought by the UK or US government - with no scruples.

Just wondering. How would it be if they put the people first? Forget the Mercs, forget the jets and the 4x4s and build one good road at a time. That will surely rid the burden of buying 4x4s. Build one or two schools per region first, a clinic here and a hospital there. How does it feel to always inaugurate foreign-funded projects? How heavy is our leaders' conscience? And when they glide in the sleek limousines, do they ever feel shame and remorse like real leaders?

What leader keeps their pride when their people are beneficiaries of foreign aid? Until when?

– 16 December 2014

Leadership Our African Problem

The irony of the pervasive cost-cutting mantra and rhetoric now popular with every African regime is that the ruling class remains untouched. In any case, the ruling class will have salary increases, added benefits, privileges and have their families, including extended members in some cases, cushioned for their entire future.

Meanwhile, the downtrodden masses will have more taken away, told to tighten their poverty belts further and watch from a distance. Some will have their jobs taken away, or will have to endure stagnant salaries which would have been eroded a 1 000 times by inflation. These, the wretched of the earth, must bear the stringent and life-sapping state-induced cost-cutting measures. That reminds me of the Ghanaian writer John Hayford, who rightly said this continent's biggest problems lie with leadership.

They are so removed from the people, Hayford said, that they are looked upon as foreigners. They are driven by self-interest so excessive that their peoples' interests are forgotten – hardly different from the colonial masters. Even Kofi Annan, the former United Nations secretary general, told the then- Organisation of African Unity (now the African Union) during his tenure in 2005 that the leaders are to blame for most of this continent's problems. Annan accused the leaders, some of whom are still clinging onto power like ticks to a cow today, that they are not doing enough to invest in development.

This, Annan said, is not something others have done to us, but is something we have done to ourselves. We have mismanaged our affairs for decades, and we are suffering the accumulated effects.

And although the cost-cutting mantra has been there pre-Magufuli era, it appears more and more African leaders are shouting themselves hoarse about it.

John Magufuli, to the uninitiated, is the Tanzanian president who made headlines for his no-nonsense anti-corruption and anti-waste drives. According to Tanzanian state media, his actions increased the monthly revenue from 900 billion shillings (N$6,4 billion) to 1,5 trillion shillings (N$10, 6 billion) within his first 100 days in office.

While Magufuli did well in containing corruption and unnecessary expenditure, his greatest challenge is creating wealth. The cuts he initiated only mopped up what was being wasted.

They are not, by any means, a vehicle for creating wealth.

Granted that Magufuli will continue cutting costs, he will be just transferring expenditure from one ministry to the next while using the same money. This is like a fine walk towards a dead-end alley. This is the same to all those imitators who, whenever they get an opportunity to mount a podium, do not waste time in shouting themselves hoarse about the importance of cutting costs.

Unashamedly, while they are preaching about cutting costs, most African leaders are busy increasing their salaries, boosting their luxury vehicle fleets, enlarging their staff complements by employing relatives and friends, and sending out their small boys to negotiate tender deals on their behalf. Most never miss an opportunity to fly out to events, which their deputies can attend, while telling the masses to be strong. It appears as if they cut from the poor and then add to their luxurious lifestyles. Most often than not, when an African leader calls for cost-cutting measures, they come up with one or other so-called scheme to improve the masses' lives.

While they are busy getting fat, the masses are told to be patient because tomorrow will bring them milk and honey. Just why can't both the leadership and the masses be patient, and wait for the milk and honey tomorrow?

I went back ever since African countries shrugged off the shroud of colonialism to see if ever any so-called scheme meant to serve the people ever worked. I found none. Only the leadership got away fatter, richer and lazier.

Those imitating Magufuli forget one thing – he never made any promises; never shouted himself hoarse; never blamed anyone; never wasted resources on conferences to plan on how to help the poor. How can you spend three times on talk shows debating strategies about job-creation and poverty alleviation as if you have just landed from Mars? Don't you know about unemployment? Haven't you heard about corruption?

Can't you see the infrastructure decay?

Those hospitals built by the colonial masters which are falling apart? Those overcrowded schools? The shrinking industries which spit workers because of a lack of state help?

Sadly, most leaders do not waste time to expound on their schemes and theories. They will never stop talking about four successful projects done with the help of foreign funders, but drop their faces once asked about the other six they failed to pull off.

African leadership lacks vision; hence the continent is always learning and starting to do things. Each new leader embarks on their phantom ideas. There is no continuation of purpose.

We are cursed with this lot.
- *5 April 2016*

Mugabe Must Stop Lying

The most dangerous enemy for Africa today is not the British, the Americans or the Europeans. These we fought, and from them, we grabbed our countries back. In any case, they cannot force themselves on Africa anymore as long as we do not want them to return. Instances where they came back, were after we had opened the doors for them.

This leaves one person – the corrupt, lying, thieving, greedy, insensitive and power-hungry African leader as the worst and most dangerous enemy of progress in Africa.

So when the new African Union chairperson, Zimbabwean president Robert Mugabe, talks about guarding against foreigners who exploit the continent's mineral wealth, he is lying. For years now, this has been Mugabe's lie premised on revenge and hatred. It has been meant to make the whole of Africa feel threatened and stand by him.

It does not matter that the AU, useless as it is, has chosen Mugabe to be its chairperson. That does not change the situation in Zimbabwe and the way Mugabe runs his Zanu-PF party as personal property. And how he deems Zimbabweans and Zimbabwe as his personal property. Strangely enough, in some quarters, Mugabe is hailed as a hero for standing up to the British and the Americans and for returning wealth to his people. Stranger still, nobody seems interested in asking why the country this champion of black empowerment rules is in the doldrums. Of course, he has told the world that sanctions imposed by the British and the Americans are to blame for his dead economy.

Of course, the British, the Americans and Europeans have transgressed against Africa but blaming them for what we could not do is carrying the blame game too far. Strangest though, Mugabe appears to have convinced those who bother listening that the imperialists caused so much suffering to his people through sanctions. And can do the same to the entire Africa.

Mugabe killed his economy from 1980 without the help of the British and American sanctions. Eight years after independence, some ministers caused the country's biggest scandal ever – the looting of the Mazda assembly plant. By 1994, it was so bad that the IMF and World Bank prescribed the economic structural adjustment programme for Zimbabwe, which required reducing government expenditure.

Mugabe initially accepted this prescription but backtracked when he could not ask his comrades to stay home. Or cut down his unbridled spending. In 1996, war veterans drove Mugabe and demanded huge payouts threatening violence. They had been ignored for years. Scared, Mugabe paid them out. The money was not budgeted for. And Zimbabwe's economy crumbled within days. The local currency that traded at 1:3 against the US dollar spiralled to 1:50 within days.

By 1998, the people had had enough. Food riots rocked the country. Realising that he had lost control of the people, Mugabe unleashed the police force. All this happened before there were any sanctions; no opposition parties, but corruption and resource mismanagement. There was no talk of empowerment and land to the poor. Mugabe was still the West's darling.

In 2000, Mugabe lost the referendum on a new constitution. Then trade union leader Morgan Tsvangirai, emboldened by the food riots and the rejection of the new constitution formed the opposition Movement for Democratic Change party.

Mugabe, considered weak by the war veterans, once again found himself in a corner. The war veterans wanted land. Mugabe still stood by the Lancaster House agreement. The referendum brought out whites in huge numbers to vote against the new constitution. They also showed open support for Tsvangirai. Mugabe was never fond of the war veterans even as their patron, but he saw them as a last political card. White-owned farms became targets.

When the first farms fell, Mugabe was abroad, and he ordered the police to drive out the invaders. But the war veterans stood their ground. And Mugabe played along with them. Because of the chaotic farm seizures, the West moved in with sanctions in 2000 long after the economy was dead.

Mugabe's tone changed. New slogans were created. Black empowerment took centre stage. But how stupid are Mugabe's people to run away from being empowered? Free land. Plenty jobs. Owners of mines. Just to sell brooms in neighbouring countries. Or to humiliate themselves by cleaning old people's bums miles away from home.

Why are so many of his poor people still without land in a country being hailed for giving it back to the rightful owners? And why is Zimbabwe importing GMO food today if Mugabe empowered black farmers? And why does Mugabe accept Western donor aid if nothing good can come of his former colonisers?

There were sanctions, of course, but Zimbabwe has the whole of Africa to trade with. She has China, one of the world's richest countries, to trade with. Still, the question is why the Zimbabwean economy has slid to the bottom? If we say the West, Europe and

Britain are the only countries that buy our minerals; this would mean that Zimbabwe's diamonds and gold must be heaped somewhere ready for the resumption of trading. If so, where are they?

The truth is that the poor have no land in Zimbabwe because the rich and Mugabe's close associates take everything. Just in December last year, his wife Grace evicted 200 families from a farm where she wants to rear wild animals. She has several other farms.

What empowerment is there when Mugabe's government buys Mercedes-Benz luxury cars from Germany and Ford Ranger all-weather double cabs from the US, and when he flies out of the country for medical treatment? His wife recently returned home after almost three months in the East recuperating from an "appendix operation".

The Germans and Americans do not have to be on African soil to exploit us; our leaders including Mugabe himself are doing it for them. When they do not support local industries, they siphon off our wealth elsewhere outside the continent. When they buy suits in Asia or Europe, they are externalising our African capital. They are propping up foreign economies.

The real African enemy is the greedy, corrupt, selfish, thieving, lying and insensitive African leader who thinks that once he is in power, he owns the people and the country.

- 27 February 2015

The Imperialists Among Us

We must go back to the beginning to find ourselves. Each country has to ask why they struggled for independence. Because as it is now, the paths we have followed seem to be leading us nowhere. This could probably be because most countries after independence just took off from where the colonisers had left. We took off as if there had not been anything wrong. As if we were just fighting to take over power.

Looking back today, it becomes apparent that none of us ever bothered to sit back and ask why people died fighting. Why so many sacrificed so much. The euphoria of being independent and of being led by black men blinded us to real issues that needed to be addressed before embarking on the journeys of rebuilding nations.

Again looking back today, there are no signs of nation building anywhere on the continent. There are no new paths created to bring forth a new African man and woman and child. There was not any new thinking. Each one of us proceeded along the same path where we did not want to be dragged. And we are here today. Still swearing at 'imperialists'. Here today still blaming the West and Europe. We are here today; still uncertain of the path we want to take because this path we followed blindly has not led us anywhere.

Just take a look. At independence, our leaders emerged from the bushes and moved into state houses that were bastions of oppression. Then they wasted no time in discarding the army fatigues for servile row suits. The next day, they were airborne. All this before sitting down to talk to the people. Ask them what they want. This should not mean they were not supposed to move into statc houses. Or wear suits. Even flying. The problem is that most of them moved swiftly and quickly to assume the role of emperors.

While they moved into state houses, nothing was done for those who could not move into such houses. With time, the problems grew until today when we feel and think that this continent is cursed. Today we still have leaders who drive around the countries they have been ruling for 20 years and still show surprise that informal settlements have grown. That there are still jobless people. That the roads are in bad shape.

Imagine after more than 30 years of failure to deliver; some leaders still make the same promises about jobs, housing, schools, roads and many others. Most of the things they were supposed to have dealt with when they took over power. It's as if every year is a new year. Most probably the closest we ever came to a leader who was keen to charting a new path, creating a new African child was Thomas Sankara of Burkina Faso. He stemmed out corruption. One of Africa's biggest threats ever. One of the scourges that will bury Africa if nothing is done.

Show me a president, dead or alive, in power or retired who has not been linked to a corrupt act and I will show you a man who has never been a president. But Sankara reduced ministers' salaries. High and ridiculous salaries are, like corruption in Africa, another act of selfishness on the part of those who assumed the roles of those whom they had fought. Sankara's state house was a small brick house. His clothes simple cloth garments made in Burkina Faso. And from cotton grown in Burkina Faso. He rode a bicycle. And the most expensive car he ever drove was a Renault 5.

One of his simple solutions was: Grow your food.

While today we have people who castigate imperialism while they act and live the life of an imperialist, Sankara once said: "Look at your plates when you eat. These imported grains of rice, corn, and millet — that is imperialism."

So look at your president when he complains about imperialism today. His watch. Where he goes for holidays. Where his children go for university. Those shiny shoes. That starched shirt. And the cigars, whiskeys, and suits. All imported. Foreign-made. Ask them why they cannot put in money to grow local food and industries. Create jobs in the process. Ask them why they move around with seven or six cars in an independent country? Cruising around in dark-tinted limousines from imperialist countries.

We may not have self-made cars in Africa, but we can afford to choose the cheapest. Cars not for luxury but necessity. But we can grow cotton in Africa. We have tailors in Africa. We can make clothes in Africa. Do all these things and create jobs in the process. And stop exporting jobs to 'imperialist' nations. Sankara declared once: "Let us consume only what we ourselves control!"

Looking at ourselves today, how much of our lives, economies and governments do we control? If we continue on this path, we will only create a frustrated, disillusioned, impoverished, angry and hopeless African child.

- 21 October 2014

No Rising Amid Groping and Fumbling

The story of Africa Rising is the story of an American man who found himself out of a job in 2009. Irwin Barkan of Vermont, a shopping mall developer, was thrown deep into the water when recession hit America. His business was driven into the mud.

One day while Barkan was idling at home, he learnt about how Wal-Mart had struck gold by investing in Mass-Mart in Africa. In Namibia, Wal-Mart now owns Game. With a friend, Morley Gordon, Barkan checked the African map for a place to go. They stumbled upon Ghana where another American company, Kosmos Energy, from Dallas had struck offshore oil.

The two took a two-week holiday in Ghana and declared later: I knew Africa was where my future was. In 2012, Barkan moved to Ghana and registered a property company called BGI that is building one of Ghana's most modern and biggest malls – Mallam Junction in Accra. The mall will open for business next year*. It will have more than 100 stores and a three-star hotel. He is also developing another mall in Kumasi.

Today, Barkan says Africa was like Asia 30 years ago. And that Africa is where action will be for the next 30 years. He has not started making money yet, but he says he will make lots of money.

This is a true story.

The story of Africa Rising is the story of an old man who was robbed of his pay cheque every Friday on his way home. A gang of robbers would wait for him at the same place along the same road and take the money. Frustrated, the old man changed places where he hid the money, but the robbers would search him and find it. One day, the old man bought a loaf of bread, made a hole and stuffed the money in it. He then walked home along the same road.

Like every other pay day, the robbers were there at the same spot. Emerging from the bushes, the robbers did not search the old man for money but snatched away the bread instead. They were hungry, they said. They had robbed enough money for the day, and the bread would do. They told the old man that he was lucky he would take his money home in as many months.

This is not a true story.

So what? You may ask. Well, Africa's rising cannot be measured by the number of foreign companies that see opportunities in the suffering of Africans. It cannot be measured by the amount of trade – skewed in favour of the foreign trader. And it cannot be measured by jobs that can only afford Africans poverty wages – jobs at shopping malls where mothers slave away as packers, cleaners, till operators and toilet cleaners.

And by the end of the day, they go home with barely enough to see them through to the next pay day. The fact is that they will live a life of a slave. There is no hope of ever owning a house or enjoying the other luxuries ordinary people elsewhere enjoy. They become 'extraordinary' human beings.

Africa can never rise if her children have nothing to show for it. What rising will this be if more and more Africans are sinking deeper and deeper into poverty? What rising is this which sees more and more informal settlements sprouting like mushrooms after the first rains? What rising is this that leaves the continent with more failed graduates? There is no rising on a continent that relies heavily on foreign aid. There is no rising on a continent that cannot provide for its children. There is no rising on a continent that is still ravaged by useless wars over which tribe is more superior to the other. There is no rising on a continent that boasts of having everything but still is unable to utilise the resources for her people. There is no rising for a continent that cannot call the shots in as far as trade is concerned.

Like the old man whose pay cheque is taken away by robbers every week, Africa walks the same path it has been walking for more than 50 years. Buying into strange ideologies (just switching pockets where to hide the pay cheque). And still losing a fortune each time.

Africa has not had any ideology to sustain economic policies that would make this rising real. She has been groping and fumbling for an ideological foothold. Each time, wasting time and resources. Changing but remaining the same.

Christine Lagarde, the International Monetary Fund managing director, summed up what Africa should do to rise – build infrastructure, build institutions and build people. Look around you wherever you are today, right now – is Africa doing this?

The chant for Africa's rising is coming from outside the continent when it should come from within for it is us who must bear testimony to this shift. Until then, Africa will forever walk the same path and lose money to the same gang of thieves regardless of where it is hidden.

Africa has not and is not only being neglected by those powers that once colonized her but by her leaders too. The revolutionary parties that promised people milk and honey in the land of Canaan have also subjected the same people to inhumane experiences. In some case, such treatment and suffering brought about by some revolutionary parties are worse than what the people went through during the colonial times. In other words, the revolutionary leader who emerged with so many promises and gave so much hope to the people turned a monster that tortured, maimed and killed the people.

The freedoms that were promised evaporated the moment some revolutionary leaders walked into the state house and were surrounded by an army of soldiers 24/7 as if there was an imminent threat. This was followed by rampant theft of national wealth and the abuse of resources. It's not only Africa in geographical terms that have been dying slowly but the people on this continent that have enough resources for everybody. And the worst part is that this situation is left to go unchallenged and unattended.

One thing though is that we are not a hopeless people and we have the future to make right. There is also the youth to put our hopes on. But the question is when will those who are clinging to power continue to do so, while we wait for future to make things right for us?

- 27 January 2015

Our Comrades Are Raping Us

It must be very difficult to run a country. At least if one judges from what happens in Africa. The leaders do not buy food. They don't pay rent. They don't fuel cars. In some cases, they have clothes bought for them. Their children's school fees are paid for them. They fly around the world without paying a cent. Their families are respected. We have even opted to call their broods first families. Their wives are first ladies. We do not call our mothers, wives, sisters or aunts first ladies. Yes, the leaders come first every time and everywhere. They cannot run the countries for us.

We give them mansions. And armed men and women to keep them safe. We also give them several servants to do everything for them. To take their children to school. Keep their children safe. In some cases, their mothers, sisters and brothers get the same special treatment. We do all this so that they can rule us well. They still cannot do it properly. We have even been kind to let their children join the ruling elite. Sometimes their wives to have joined the ruling queue. And cousins. And sisters, hoping that they can do a better job.

But just why they cannot do a proper job of it is baffling. These who eat free. Sleep free. Lead an everything-paid-for life. But still, fail just to do a better job of ruling us.

We have accepted their sarcasm of them being our servants even when we know what this means. For what servant lives like a king while the king lives like a servant? On the streets. In informal settlements. Thirsty. Hungry. In the dust.

So if we do all these things for them: starve to death for them; brave the cold for them; walk thousands of kilometres for them; work for them; compose songs in their honour; sing and dance for their visitors, just why can't they do one thing – rule us well?

This is not a joke or an exaggeration, comrades. It's not made up. Just take a look at us today. Look at Africa despite piling years of being independent; most remain jobless. Homeless. Waterless. Powerless. Impoverished. Diseased. Divided. Brutalised. Uncertain. Our youths flee the continent in droves. Some die on the high seas. Others make it to Europe for self-enslavement. Our women too give up everything for livelihood. Those who remain on the homeland are drunkards given up to fate. The active ones steal from us.

This is not a fixation with the negative. It could be happening elsewhere too, but for and in Africa it is worse. Just check:

What good has come out of Ethiopia? The great Haile Selassie's country. Look at Egypt. The land of the Pharaohs. The cradle of civilisation. Morocco – the land of beauty. Somalia – the land of the Gods. The Central African Republic – the land of Ubangi-Shari. Liberia – the land of freedom. The Congo has remained just that – the land of misery. Ghana – the land of gold but some of her children are running away. Mali – the land of the Dogon. Niger – the land of fear. Nigeria – the giant of Africa, now staggering under the heavy load of violence. Chad – the land of broken hearts. Malawi - the Warm Heart of Africa. The Sudan – the broken land. Check Zambia, Zimbabwe, Uganda, Angola, Namibia and South Africa.

Either all these countries are already in the mud, or they are rushing there, determined. Others are trying hard to crawl out, but they can't make it. This is all because the people we feed, clothe, house, protect, respect and sacrifice for are not returning the favours. They demand more even when they see we have nothing more but our pain and shame to give.

This is not about Europe. Or America. Or even China anymore, comrades. It's not about the former colonisers. It is about us. We have everything to do with us. If we allow Europe to come in after we asked her to leave, we have ourselves to blame. If we open our doors to China, we should not cry foul when China takes over everything.

This is our fate. All of us on the motherland. Our paths run into each other. It's a shared destiny. It is as if this fate runs in the Nile, the Zambezi, the Limpopo and the Orange. Flowing with the tide from the north to the south, from the east to the west. As if the people whom we feed, clothe, house and protect are children of the same mother. Why do we feed, clothe, house and protect them when they rape us? Steal from us as if what we give is not enough? Deny us jobs, education, health, shelter, promised freedoms? It's like we are feeding them so that they can get strength to overpower us. And rape us.

But just why can't they be faithful to us and do that one simple thing – rule us properly? Is it that difficult to do? Now, comrades, is it too much to ask to be ruled well?

- 29 July 2014

The Sanctions Myth in Zimbabwe

It's true that Zimbabwe is besieged today and has been for years now. But it's not true that we could not have, if we wanted, set ourselves free. Sanctions are real – targeted or not – but they are breakable. And Zimbabwe can and could have broken them. So it's a myth that all our problems today are sanctions-made.

Maybe to understand this, one has to go back to as early as the 1990s when the economy started but slowly to give in.

It's a fact that at independence in 1980, Zimbabwe spent a lot of money in health, education and various other sectors to bridge gaps created by an unfair and unjust system. Spending on education rose from Z$227,6m in 1979 to Z$628m in 1990 while health expenditure went up from Z$66,4m to Z$188,6m. An enormous public service sector subsidies, the 10-year involvement in the Mozambican civil war from 1982 to 1992 and then subsequent drought years further debilitated the economy such that by mid-90s prices had become unstable. The budget operated at a deficit and taxes became high. This drove public debt higher.

To recover lost economic growth, the government accepted the Enhanced Economic Structural Advancement Programme (Esap) in 1991. The programme that ended in 1995 meant that all subsidies had to go; public enterprises either be nationalised or privatised to enhance growth; streamline government by cutting down on expenditure.

Esap was supposed to be a short term programme that would first snuff out some jobs to create more. But it did not work. The privatisation or nationalisation of PEs without better management led to further decline in productivity. The government did not reduce expenditure. No jobs were created. And deficit went further up. Instability chipped in.

A few black business people operating as advocates for black empowerment demanded their entitlements and government acknowledged them by giving contracts and concessional loans. This further puts pressure on government forcing it to borrow domestically thereby causing even more instability. Consumer prices skyrocketed.

Under Esap, government was also forced to fall into heavy debt, and international donors refused to write off the debts because the Zimbabwean government had failed to honour its part of the deal. After the failure of Esap, government cooked up the Zimbabwe Programme for Economic and Social Transformation (Zimprest) in 1996. Zimprest was supposed to be implemented by government, business, labour and civil society through the National Consultative Forum (NECF).

Although Zimprest was promising in the first two years when growth reached 7%, the depreciation of the Z$ because of low tobacco and minerals' prices hit the economy hard. This was followed by a disastrous 1997/ 98 rainfall season. Inflation took its toll, and most industries did not perform as expected.

One major event that drove the economy onto to its knees was the ex-combatants' payouts in 1997 when government was forced to fork out Z$4b as compensation to former freedom fighters. Since the money had not been budgeted for, the Z$ lost with a record 72% against the US$ and the stock market crashed by 46% on 14 November 1997 signalling the economic meltdown that is still haunting the country today. The payouts depleted foreign reserves which according to Kingdom Financial Holdings statistics at the time fell from US$760m early 1997 to US$255m by November of the same year. This exposed the local currency which at the time was worth US$1,315. The Reserve Bank of Zimbabwe was also exposed because it meant that with such low foreign reserves, it could only underwrite imports for a month. Government's debt in 1997 was more than $60 billion, and it was estimated that servicing the debt cost more than a billion a month. Servicing this debt ate into resources that could otherwise have been channelled towards education and health which started to decline.

In response to the crisis, the government increased bread, sugar, soft drinks, commuter fares, milk and mealie meal prices and the consumers rioted in protest.

As if that was not enough, Zimbabwe was sucked into the DRC civil war in 1998 resulting in the IMF and several other donors suspending financial assistance.

By 1999, it was clear that the economy was heading south. The final nail was the haphazard takeover of farms by ex-combatants as part of their demands. This drove agricultural input down.

With the birth of the Movement for Democratic Change (MDC) and political violence, economic sanctions – the Zimbabwe Democracy and Economic Recovery Act (Zidera) - were imposed in 2001 by the US. This meant no loan extensions, no credit guarantees and no debt reduction or cancellation. The fact is that the sanctions came to haunt an already battered economy and in a bid to revive the economy, Gideon Gono was appointed the RBZ governor in 2003.

This is the man who could have saved Zimbabwe had all the money he gave out been utilised for the benefit of the nation at large. His policies are not in any way different from those of US president George Bush and his successor Barack Obama and indeed other government elsewhere. The only difference is that Gono's biggest enemy was corruption. Most of the people who received money, diesel or machinery from the central bank misused them. Up to now, there has not been any audit to bring to book people who squandered the resources.

The other factor was that some Zanu-PF members thought they were entitled to enjoy the gifts from the reserve bank while the opposition stood by - criticising.

In an interview two years ago, Gono admitted that his programmes failed because of farm under-utilisation and disruptions; rampant corruption; indiscipline as well as lack of law and order.

So this sanctions beat is like repeating the same lie over and over again until we start believing it.

Maybe the start would be dealing with corruption.

– March 2013

The Fourth Estate in a quandary

J ournalism, the so-called Fourth Estate, has been and still is an extension of Zimbabwe's problems either by misinforming the people or misleading the government. It's a fact that even today media in Zimbabwe is polarised. One can safely say there are four distinct media groupings in the country today.

The first group is made up of state media journalists; that is the Zimpapers stable while the second group consists of the so-called independent media with the third group being those who use the new media – internet journalists. The fourth group is the journalist-cum-civic worker.

The situations the three groups of journalists create reminds me of the Biblical books Mathew, John, Luke and Mark who all wrote about Jesus Christ's life as eye witnesses but give varying versions of what happened or did not happen. But before delving deeper into what and how each of these groups has done to our country, I will dissect them.

The state media journalist has been the laughing stock. The other groups view them as unable, suckers and inept. This, to some extent, is true. There is some deadwood at Zimpapers. There are 'senior journalists' who have been with the Zimpapers stable for more than ten years now. Most can't write a feature or think about any topic except when it comes to reporting events. These are the 'The President said...' type or the 'The Minister stated in a statement . . . '

In fact, such 'senior journalists' haven't matured professionally but have remained reporters. It's understandable because in their minds they think they have no mandate to think beyond what they are fed. It is for this reason that the state media journalist is laughed at. I remember when I was at The Herald asking a close journalist friend after MDC-T's parliamentary majority win why he can't for once advise Zanu-PF constructively, properly? He did, for once, write such an article pointing out where and why Zanu-PF had lost and would continue to lose. But for the majority, every day is just another day and years have piled up. Being a journalist has become just a routine. There is no creativity and no personal development. What matters to most of them is the pay packet. That's why at Zimpapers you find journalists who have been there for 20 years or more yet they can't show why they have been there. These are the nameless and faceless By Herald Reporter type. For those who have the chance to accompany the President, staying at Zimpapers has been good for them. Life goes on, and they die professionally like babies sleeping during feeding time.

The second group is the so-called independent media journalist. Most of them walk with confidence and view themselves as masters of the pen. They dominate any discussions and act as if they have sources in high places. They boast about their stories and believe that everything the government does is wrong and should be criticised except, of course, Reserve Bank Governor Gideon Gono. The most distressing fact is that even where these journalists should be independent to criticise, evaluate, assess and dissect issues, all they do at best is inflate issues by giving unbalanced reports.

It's a fact that during the rise of the MDC, these journalists never looked at the other side of the coin and wrote about the intra-party violence that later led to the party's first split. It's not true that they did not know about it, but they covered up all this. They also ignored or did not take former Highfield MDC MP, Munyaradzi Gwisai's worries when he quit the party citing loss of direction and a deviation from the founding goals and aspirations. Maybe, the only fair comment one read was Joram Nyathi's column where he maturely dealt with issues but that made him very unpopular and some quarters called for his head. It was delivered just like King Herod delivered John the Baptist's head on a platter. Even here, one finds nothing much except criticism, mostly unfair, unbalanced and unresearched. Even here one would read between the lines what information has been taken out.

The cyber journalist has been and is the most viral type because they operate like flies – nameless, faceless and devoid of any ethics. This type has the entire wide world to lie, scorn, deride and rebuke sometimes innocent people.

Indeed, they get away with it.

For them anything is news. Get a fake comment here and throw a name there, hey presto the story is ready to go. These have cost the country enormously. Even legislation has not been able to reach and sniff them out. Maybe, such a situation was created by the closure of media houses in Zimbabwe. But it appears this group, with the establishment of newspapers in the country, is facing extinction like the Zim dollar.

The fourth group is made of those who used the profession as a spring board to achieve their political aspirations. Some are now within party structures where they hold high positions while others have made money as civic leaders or activists. It is within this group where democracy is a buzz word such that life is nothing but about democracy. For and to them, life starts and ends with democracy.

But once some of them get the positions they want, they then turn against democracy.

The fifth groups consist of those who openly declare their allegiance to political parties and vow to write in defence of whatever such parties say regardless of whether it helps the majority or destroys them. These are not only found in the Zimpapers stable but across the spectrum.

We have exacerbated the Zimbabwean problem by being dishonest to the profession. We lie and panel beat issues to suit our needs. In the process, we have become activists. Our duty to inform reasonably, to act as the people's watchdogs have been discarded either for money or self-glory. While we use the word democracy, our actions do not show any democratic thinking. Yes, the Zimbabwean fourth estate is in distaste.

— February 2012

Cecil the Lion Sleeps Tonight

The world today knows more about the Zimbabwean lion Cecil, killed by North American dentist Walter Palmer, than they do about the Zimbabwean journalist and human rights activist Itai Dzamara, who has been missing since 9 March 2015.

Zimbabwe's President Robert Mugabe on August 10 criticised the killing of Cecil, saying the animal was an essential part of the country's heritage. Our wildlife, all our animals, belongs to us.

"They should not be shot with a gun or with an arrow", Mugabe told thousands who gathered at a shrine on the outskirts of the capital Harare to commemorate Heroes' Day. "Even Cecil the Lion is yours. He is dead. He was yours to protect and he [was] there to keep you safe."

Cecil was lured from the Hwange National Park and then shot with a bow before he was finished off with a gun. His head was cut off, and skin is taken away as trophies. Cecil left 13 cubs and a brother Jericho. Dzamara was abducted in broad daylight from a barbershop in Glen View, one of Harare's densely populated suburbs. He was abducted by five men driving an Isuzu double cab. He left behind a young wife and two small children.

In October last year, Dzamara closed down his newspaper and wrote to Zimbabwe's President Robert Mugabe asking him to step down and save the country from further decay. He delivered a letter to Mugabe's office and then started what is now known as the Occupy Africa Unity Square movement. Africa Unity Square is opposite the Zimbabwean parliament and close to Mugabe's offices in Harare.

While Cecil's "murder" is unforgivable, it is sad that the media never raised its voice high for the abduction of Dzamara as is being done for Cecil. Experts even gave the world a blow-by-blow account of life in the jungle. Even the Zimbabwean government has called for the extradition of the American dentist to stand trial where he committed the offence. Although the details leading to Cecil's "murder" are not clear at this moment, what happened to Dzamara before his abduction is known.

Dzamara was abducted after he had attended a Movement for Democratic Change (MDC-T) rally on March 8 in Harare where he called on Mugabe to go. Most probably, that was the last straw for his abductors after they had failed to break his spirit through assault and detentions. The abduction came after a contingent of 20 police officers armed with batons assaulted Dzamara and members of his movement in November last year. That attack resulted in him being hospitalised.

The second attack was carried out by members of the war veterans association, who held Dzamara and two others captive in the basement of the Zimbabwe African National Union-Patriotic Front (ZANU-PF) headquarters in Harare, while Mugabe was holding a meeting upstairs. In between, Dzamara and a few brave activists were subjected to beatings and arrests which did not amount to anything since the police could not prove any case against them.

But Dzamara returned to the square each time in defiance of those who were harassing him. He spoke about a non-violent demonstration and urged the nation to stand up against Mugabe's rule.

So far, there have been mixed reactions to Dzamara's abduction from the Zimbabwean government with some ZANU-PF members accusing the MDC-T of stage managing the kidnapping. Mugabe's spokesperson even said his boss was not bothered by Dzamara's disappearance while the state-run media has been trying to paint the disappearance as a non-issue. Only recently, the police offered a US$10 000 reward for information on Dzamara's whereabouts. Even the courts ordered the cops to put more effort in searching for the missing activist, but just last week the officer in charge of the search told the courts that they had drawn a blank.

Interestingly, the officer in charge of the search was involved in the abduction of another activist, Jestina Mukoko, from her home just outside Harare at around 5h00 on December 3, 2008. For days, Mukoko's whereabouts were unknown. The government denied any knowledge of her whereabouts. Even a High Court order compelling the government to release Mukoko was ignored.

It took former US president Jimmy Carter, former UN secretary general Kofi Annan and South Africa's former first lady Graca Machel's intervention for the government to admit that they were holding Mukoko.

Apart from Dzamara and Mukoko as well as many others who just disappeared in the silence of the night because they are not high profile figures, there is the case of Rashiwe Guzha, a typist within the secret service who disappeared in May 1990. There is also the case of an army captain, Edwin Nleya, who disappeared in 1989 shortly after threatening to expose commanders who were involved in ivory smuggling and the death of more than 500 elephants in Mozambique.

Amnesty International said Nleya had stumbled upon the poaching information when Zimbabwe was helping Mozambique fight Renamo. Nleya's case is told in a report titled Poaching and Unexplained Death: The Case of Captain Nleya that was published 1992.

In 2000, Patrick Nabayana, a polling agent for an MDC candidate was abducted by men armed with AK47s and his body was found some months later. In February 2012, activist Paul Chizuzu was abducted. He has not been found.

All these cases never broke the Internet, and today the world knows more about Cecil the lion than it does about Itai Dzamara, who turned 35 on August 8.

- August 11, 2015

Packaging the African leader

Ever since March 5 1957 when the Gold Coast attained independence and Kwame Nkrumah became the first prime minister declaring that his country's independence was incomplete as long as the rest of Africa remained colonised, the west sought ways of packaging African leaders. Packaging meant that a leader had to adhere to the norms, descriptions and definition according to the west and former colonial masters.

In the early years before civic organisations became snipers in the name of democracy, the west used coups to depose leaders who defied packaging. In almost every coup that happened in Africa, there was the hand of the CIA or FBI. In the early days, such interference was for keeping Russian influence off the continent. So any new leader who showed affection for socialism or communism was overthrown through a coup.

As a result, there were 14 major coups between 1963 and 1966 while by 1968; the number had risen to 64 attempted and successful coups on the continent. This does not mean that African leaders had no problems with their own conduct towards their people. There were various issues which could, if it was today, be passed on as undemocratic. But all these issues did not matter to the US, the British or the French.

In Togo, for example, Sylvanus Olympio was seen as a threat for his grassroots approach to issues while in Belgian Congo (DRC) Patrice Lumumba emerged as a communist and Nkrumah had to go because of his support for and discontent with Lumumba's assassination. Milton Obote of Uganda rubbed the British on the wrong side with his proposals to nationalise foreign businesses as well as voicing grave concern with British's plans to sell arms to apartheid South Africa. In those early days, it was not about democracy, economic mismanagement or human rights – it was purely to protect business interests.

Togo and President Sylvanus Olympio

The most interesting is the story of a small West African country, Togo which gained independence in 1961 from the French. A trade unionist called Sylvanus Olympio was elected the first president but by 1963, he was assassinated in a coup. This became the first bloody coup in Africa. It will not surprise that Olympio was murdered when he went to seek refuge in the American embassy compound which was close to the presidential palace.

Reports say that after he had sent his family to safety, Olympio climbed the wall into the embassy compound but found the door locked. He then hid in one of the cars where the US ambassador found him and went away promising to come back with keys to the door. But before his return, Olympio was discovered by a 27-year-old army sergeant Gnassingbe Eyadema who later became one of Africa's most notorious leaders. It's strongly suspected that the US ambassador alerted his French counterpart who in turn reported Olympio's whereabouts to the military.

But just like any other military man during the first era of coups, Eyadema handed over power to Nicolas Grunitzky who was Olympio's brother-in-law. Togo has never known peace since then. In 1969, Eyadema overthrew Grunitzky and took over power until his death in 2005.

Belgian Congo and Patrice Lumumba

Africa's saddest story is that of Patrice Lumumba, Belgian Congo's first Prime Minister who was ousted from office in 1960 three months after inauguration. This was a coup by proxy where Joseph Mobutu, a chief of staff officer appointed by Lumumba caused the murder of his boss with the help of the US and Belgium. Mobutu, just like Eyadema, Mobuto gave power to Joseph Kasavubu whom he overthrew in 1965.

Lumumba's crime was giving a speech saying he would make sure that his country's resources would be for the Congolese. It was an unprepared speech which caused a stir in Belgium and the US. It was at the height of the Cold War era and the West was keen to keep down all African leaders who showed any leanings to Russia. Mobutu, who also became one of Africa's worst leaders, ruled Congo until he was ousted by Laurent Kabila in 1997.

Ghana and Kwame Nkrumah

Ghana was the first African country to attain independence in 1957 but by 1966, Kwame Nkrumah had been overthrown. Like Lumumba, Nkrumah had a dream of changing Africa by helping free every colonised country. One of his most popular speeches delivered on 5 March 1957 was:

We are going to see that we create our African personality and identity. We again rededicate ourselves in the struggle to emancipate other countries in Africa; for our independence is meaningless unless it is linked up with the total liberation of the African continent.

But when he voiced his concern over the assassination of Lumumba in 1960, Nkrumah made the US unhappy. A journal called InformAfrica which publishes news and information that influence Africa says the coup that overthrew Nkrumah was engineered by the US, the British and the French. Quoting a leaked US Foreign Policy report titled *Cases by Intervention Node; a US Foreign Policy in Perspective*, InformAfrica says President John Kennedy offered military training to junior officers to prepare them for any possibilities including a coup because Nkrumah had taken an 'ugly lurch to the left'. The report notes that the CIA was pressured to come up with a 'well-conceived and executed action programme' of economic and diplomatic pressure designed to 'induce a chain reaction eventually leading to Nkrumah's downfall'. US ambassador to Ghana, the report further says, described Nkrumah as 'a badly confused and immature person'.

"Over the next year, the security forces, who were becoming increasingly dissatisfied with Nkrumah, were cultivated by both the US and the British. By February 1965, the CIA was receiving word of coup plotting, an issue raised explicitly by the US ambassador with the CIA director the next month," says the report.

Rumour of a coup involving 'key military and police figures' materialising spread in May 1965, the report says adding, "The plotters were keeping us briefed and State thinks we're more on the inside than the British. While we're not directly involved, we and other Western countries (including France) have been helping to set up the situation by ignoring Nkrumah's pleas for economic aid."

However, the May coup did not happen thereby angering junior officers trained in the US to act with the help of the CIA to eventually depose Nkrumah in 1966 while he was on a visit to China. This time, the army guys who spearheaded the coup did not hand it over to civilians. Lt Gen Joseph Arthur Ankrah took over as head of State until 1969.

Uganda, Idi Amin and the British

Idi Amin of Uganda once boasted that the British made him what he was. Indeed, it was the British who gave him power when they were scared with Milton Obote's policies which were viewed as detrimental to their interest. Mark Curtis in his book *Unpeople: Britain's Secret Human Rights Abuses* says declassified files says British officials were 'delighted to see the back of the government of Milton Obote', Uganda's President who was overthrown by Idi Amin Dada in 1971. Obote's crimes' list, Curtis notes, were read out by British High Commissioner to Kampala then, Richard Slatter who accused him of making policies detrimental to British interests in Uganda. Some of the crimes were nationalisation plans and the threat to withdraw from the Commonwealth in protest to Britain's plan to sell arms to apartheid, South Africa. Curtis says,

> The Obote government's public challenge to British interests on arms was matched by its nationalisation decrees. In May 1970 Obote announced legislation whereby the government would take over all import and export businesses and acquire compulsorily 60% of the shares of oil companies, manufacturing industries, banks, insurance companies and other sectors. Compensation would be paid over periods of up to 15 years out of the profits received and paid over to the Ugandan government as the major shareholder.

Quoting a British Foreign Office official, Curtis writes; ". . . There is a danger that other countries will be tempted to try and get away with similar measures with more damaging consequences for British investment and trade." According to Curtis, a British business lobby group, the East African and Mauritius Association advised the Foreign Office that if they let Obote get away with his plans, British investments overseas would be lost. "The result is the loss of British investments overseas and the establishment of precedents which could involve similar action by governments of other territories with adverse repercussions on the British economy."

Indeed, Curtis says Sudan nationalised some of the foreign businesses soon after Obote's announcement and this prompted the British to move fast. Britain had about 50 companies in Uganda. There were banks such as Standard, Barclays and Grindlays, Shell/BP, BAT, Dunlop, Brooke Bond and Mackenzie Dalgety among others.

Amin who was the Army Chief of Staff ironically deposed Obote while he was attending a Commonwealth conference in Singapore. The first country to recognise Amin's government was Britain, the US and Israel while African states could not immediately accept Amin. A British Foreign Office statement then said, "Our interest in Uganda regarding citizens, investment, trade and aid programme [sic] are best served in these circumstances by early recognition."

In his statement, British Assistant Under Secretary of State at the Foreign Office, Harold Smedley said, "We have no cause to shed tears on Dr Obote's departure. At long last, we have a chance of placing our relations with Uganda on a friendly footing." And British High Commissioner to Kampala, Slater wrote to the Foreign Office saying, "Anglo-Ugandan relations can only benefit from the change. Amin is deeply grateful (as I am) for the promptness with which Her Majesty's Government recognised his regime."

Also, Curtis says, British officials 'canvassed' other moderate African governments, "We are hoping that we can discreetly let General Amin know of these efforts which we are making on his behalf." The British knew about Amin's recklessness and involvement in unexplained murders in the army. They ignored all this because for and to them, he was the right candidate to do the dirty job.

— *9 September 2011 (The Southern Times)*

Humanity is Under Threat

We are living in a turbulent time. A loveless time. A dangerous time. A confusing time. A harrowing time. This is a crossroad. And it appears we are lost while searching for ourselves. Why can't we find answers to the violence? Workshop after workshop. Threats after threats. One women's group after another women's group. Long jail term after another long jail term. Prayer after prayer. Statistics and figures, scenarios and debates. All that is yet to yield any results. The violence is not relenting.

If it is not an angry partner battering their lover to death or into ugly unsightly wounds, then it is a young overwhelmed mother throwing away their baby. Dumping nine months of what should be a positive life-changing. Nine months of carrying a life, a soul, a generation. But for such young mothers, it is throwing away nine months of agony, anger, shame and unforgivable experience. Research and castigation. Still, nothing has changed. Where are we going wrong? Where are we losing ourselves?

Many have sought refuge in becoming religious zealots just to shut out the anger in the world, to experience a semblance of normalcy, and to be humane. They have become so obsessed with and absorbed in their welfare. They try hard to isolate themselves from the turbulent time we are all living in today. But that appears to have failed too because what afflicts us today is our hearts. The anger, the sadness, the unforgiving, the despair, the avenging spirits, and the coldness are all in our hearts. We carry these wherever we go, and with time, they seek to escape from us.

What is not in our hearts any more is love, kindness, affection, respect for one another – in short, we have lost our humanity. This is why these times we are living in are dangerous times.

Once, people lived like people. With so much love and respect for each. They were united by humanity. And all this did not need workshops. It did not need religion. It did not need research. It did not need threats because humanity is as natural as the rising sun. Or the falling of the rain. Or the coming of winter.

Our search, therefore, should start with man and woman – the parents. These are the microcosm of humanity, the foundation stones for the society. They are brought together by love and affection. They bring forth children who should be symbols of their love and affection. These are the people who should help heal the world, end the anger, and spread the love.

But if you look around today, this set-up does not exist. Most are themselves products of a vicious circle of emptiness resulting from either the absence of a father or a mother. Most of them are incomplete individuals whose foundations are set on one stone yet humanity, and the society should depend on these half-baked adults still sweltering in anger. Religion cannot stand in for a missing parent. Education falls short of endowing love and compassion. Wealth too cannot fill hearts with love and affection just like what the Dalai Lama says.

He says there is no need for temples and that religion should be simple. He also says there is no need for complicated philosophy because: 'Your mind, your own heart is the temple. Your philosophy is simple kindness. Again if you look around, simple kindness and compassion are in short supply. Once again, the Dalai Lama says without love, compassion and kindness 'humanity cannot survive'.

This is why government leaders and many other people are disturbed by the unrelenting violence; why researchers are working full throttle; why there are so much anger, so much despair and so much hopelessness. Our hearts are empty. Our minds are wandering in emptiness. Our lives are one big yawn – whether you have lots of money or your pockets are holed. Writing to the Corinthians, Paul sets the rules which, if we apply them, can bring us back our humanity. He says of the three things – faith, hope and love – that will last forever 'the greatest of these is love'. Note that he does not talk about being a convert to any religious sect for one to be able to love, to have hope and to be faithful. To be kind and respectful. 'If I gave everything I have to the poor and even sacrificed my body, I could boast about it; but if I didn't love others, I would have gained nothing,' Paul says.

Maybe, the starting point today is to teach our children how to love, to care and to be kind. We should start working on restoring the microcosm of humanity and society – the family unit. Of course, there are families today from where hopeless children come. This is because such families are just a form without any functions. Such families have become crucibles where angry children, devoid of love, kindness, compassion and respect are formed.

8 July 2014

I hate democracy.

Whatever it is, democracy is a very strange animal!
It is very selfish and full of itself. It does not have
time to listen to others. It has no room for those who
see and think differently. It lashes out, threatens and punishes
divergent voices and minds.

Nothing must exist besides itself. It must have full control and
authority to deride, chide, censure and castigate those seen as not
conforming to whatever shape, colour or size of this democracy is. It
has taken it upon itself to carry out acts for which it castigates
others. It is for this democracy to kill but howls when others kill. It
stereotypes nations and people and places them in small boxes as if
they are blood samples of a virus. The small boxes are then labelled:
operatives, apologists, dictators, bum lickers, hangers-on, notorious,
fiends, torturers and murderers etc. etc. etc.

While in democracy, violence is and should be condemned, this
version does not leave anything to chance but makes sure that
nothing will remain standing once it's done. This democracy speaks
the language of anger and hatred. It seeks to isolate and shame all
those who do not agree in principle with whatever desires or wishes
such democracy wants. It is God in itself. Everything must rally
around it. Stop and listen only to its voice. Every person must kneel
and crawl only to this democracy.

And many voices are drowned. Many people sit back in fear of
being called names. The debate is stifled because once you say what
you think and it's different from what democracy wants, then you
are an operative or an apologist. Whatever view you have does not

mean anything as long as it is different from theirs. So now there are rogue nations and axis of evil nations while some opposition parties have taken it upon themselves to champion democracy hence the inclusion of the word democracy in their names.

Just check this: In South Africa, there is the Independent Democratic Party; United Christian Democratic Party; United Democratic Movement; Alliance for Democracy and Prosperity; Alliance of Free Democrats and Christian Democratic Alliance. In Botswana, you find the Botswana Democratic Party; Botswana Movement for Democracy; New Democratic Front while Malawi has Alliance for Democracy; Malawi Democratic Party; Movement for Genuine Democratic Change; National Democratic Alliance and United Democratic Front. Zambia has Movement for Multiparty Democracy; United Democratic Alliance; Forum for Democracy and Development and National Democratic Focus. One wonders whether the inclusion of the word democracy means what it is supposed to say or it's a façade.

In simple terms, democracy is doing what is right. It is about respect; about love; about fostering peace and there should not be any rewards for being good to others. But the world, of course, is more complicated than this simple definition of democracy. It got its ways of redefining things. Democracy's holier than thou attitude is like that of religion. While religion is supposed to foster understanding, harmony and peace among the peoples of the world, what it has done so far is cause wars, massacres and evils that make Satan green with envy.

If religion were tolerant, 9/11 would not have happened. If religion were tolerant, there would not be the Israel/ Palestine problem. If religion were tolerant, Nigeria would be at peace with its peoples. If religion were tolerant, a lot of things that went wrong and are going wrong today in the name of faith would not be happening. Egypt today after putting a stable and united front, the centre has fallen apart with one spiritual side taking over for their selfish ends.

Most probably one good example of the ironies of democracy in Somalia. In 1991, Siad Barre was kicked out by a united opposition in the name of democracy. But look at Somalia today 20 years after the overthrow of Siad Barre. It's made up warring fiefdoms.

The so-called progressive forces have failed to carry the country forward because of selfishness and greed. There is no central government, and the state is divided into semi-independent clans led by warlords. All the attempts – 14 times to be precise – to set up a central government have failed. Whatever form of government there is, is just posturing because the elected representatives have no power, but the warlords do. Compare it to what it used to be under Siad Barre who was accused of despotic tendencies. At least, Siad Barre held the nation together, and Somalia was a progressive country. Somalis were better under Siad Barre's 'despotic' measures that made them secure, safe and regarded as a people with a country. Now add religion to the equation, and you get a fragmented Somalia that will never be a country again. And it is a religion that is keeping food away from some sections affected by famine. It is a religion that is supposed to be clean, understanding, selfless, caring and helpful which is killing people.

I hate democracy. I hate religion.

15 August 2011

History drowns Dr Kenneth Kaunda's voice of peace

He is now known as the weeping president and the last time he addressed the Southern African Development Community (SADC) in Windhoek a few years ago, Dr Kenneth Kaunda, former Zambian president, wept as he sang his signature tune, *Tiyende Pamodzi Ndi Mutima Umo* (Let us Walk Together with One Heart).

Seeing Dr Kaunda shed tears, it's unimaginable that this is the man who liberated southern Africa and was instrumental in pushing for the release of late South African President Nelson Mandela. It's so distant to think that the role Dr Kenneth Kaunda played can be likened to that performed by Che Guevara. But today, he has been relegated to the fringes of history such that he does not make much news as Nelson Mandela does.

Dr Kaunda was admitted in a Windhoek hospital for what was termed a 'routine check', and that event did not send headlines across the world screaming as did Mandela's hospitalisation for another 'routine check' a few months ago. There are 99% chances that if one asks the youth who Dr Kenneth Kaunda is, they would not know but mention the name Nelson Mandela, and they will tell you. This is so because Dr Kaunda fought to liberate the region by accommodating revolutionary movements in his country when Zambia attained independence in 1964.

While democracy is keyword today, Dr Kaunda's role as a liberator and proponent of democracy never has and will never be recognised because he helped in taking over power from those favoured by the west. If the Kaunda-Mandela parallel is to be drawn further, one would conclude that the west loves Mandela today not so much because he has done anything for Africa in general or South Africa in particular but because he turned the other cheek and shook the bloodied hands of the people who murdered his children. One would also conclude that the west packaged Mandela for the world in the same way they package products such as cigarettes, coke cola, and alcohol as well as clothing brands for consumption. It is for this reason that no other African statesmen who reached out their hand to help others survive the onslaught of the west will ever be accorded the same respect and marketing Mandela receives.

All that we have seen and got are street names after Dr Kaunda with a municipality in South Africa in the North West Province changing its name form Southern District Municipality to Dr Kenneth Kaunda Municipality for the man's 'invaluable contribution to the freedom struggle in Africa; outstanding leadership; peace and progress initiatives in Africa'.

So today Dr Kaunda who sacrificed everything – his political career, his country's economy, his life as a father and husband – for the betterment of the region lives the life of an ordinary man. Unlike other African leaders – his successor the late Frederick Chiluba for example – who leaves the State House burdened with accusations of corruption and looting of the economy, Dr Kaunda was removed with his hands clean. Most of the ministers who served in his government do not have much to show for the time they spent in government.

He is, most probably, one of the very few African leaders who stayed on in their countries when they were removed from power and continue to live like normal citizens without anyone booing them.

Likewise, Dr Kaunda's contribution to the independence of Angola, Mozambique, South Africa, Zimbabwe and Namibia has been forgotten. Nobody cares that Dr Kaunda's benevolence towards his neighbours scarred the country's economy badly and deeply. Decades of wars in the region meant that the Rhodesians and the apartheid regime in South Africa and the then South West Africa (Namibia) would from time to time bomb Zambian infrastructure causing damage that needed Dr Kaunda's government to repair. And this cost a lot for a country that survived on copper.

In an interview with Harry Kreisler, Executive Director of UC Berkeley's Institute of International Studies and Executive Producer of Conversations with History, Dr Kaunda admits this fact:

We opened our doors, and all liberation movements moved from Tanzania to Zambia. That meant being bombed from time to time by South African warplanes. Zimbabwe, Southern Rhodesia in those days, the Portuguese in Angola, the Portuguese in Mozambique, the settlers in Namibia, all these were now attacking Zambia because they wanted us to fear that accommodating liberation movements meant being bombed, bridges being destroyed; you build, they will blast them again, and so on. Oil places, where you hide your oil, they come and bomb and destroy those. This is what life then was, but it was something we had to do. When God says, 'Love thy neighbour as thyself' and 'Do unto others as you'd have them do unto you' there's no choice there if you understood that. We understood that we accepted it, we worked together.

Dr Kaunda further says his desire, and that of the people of Zambia was to see other countries free from 'people who did not believe that people of all races were God's children'.

'We were not fighting for the independence of Zambia; we were also very much concerned with seeing to it that our neighbours in that region were becoming independent. Angola, west of us; Mozambique, west of us; Zimbabwe, south of us; South West Africa (Namibia) and of course, South Africa itself...' he said. This was a good fight for Africa but not for the west, and Dr Kaunda became target number one. When Dr Kaunda took in liberation movements, Dr Kamuzu Banda of Malawi declined to have anything to do with the plight of others. The late Julius Nyerere noted this in his introduction to a book titled *Kenneth Kaunda of Zambia: The times and the Man* written by the Irish missionary Fergus Macpherson:

If Kenneth Kaunda and the people of Zambia had decided that it was too difficult, like Dr Banda in Malawi had done, we would not participate in the struggle.' President Nyerere wrote, 'We all would have understood that this was the right thing for him and the people of Zambia to do. They went ahead because they believed in what they were doing.

But to understand Dr Kaunda better – to know the depth and width of heart – has to go back into his childhood where he used music as a weapon to get through to the people. Born at Lubwa Mission Station in 1924 as one of eight children, his father, Reverend David Kaunda of the Church of Scotland endowed in him the gift of love not only for his close family members but all races.

His parents also taught him to read at an early age such that by the time he started school at Munali in Lusaka, young Kaunda was ahead of his peers. After Munali where he got a teaching certificate, young Kaunda took up a teaching post at Chinsali Mission when the winds of change driven by the late Dr Banda and another Zambian nationalist leader Harry Nkumbula were rising against the Federation of Southern Africa. At 25, Kaunda took up the campaign holding solo guitar sessions across Zambia (then Northern Rhodesia) singing freedom songs and created branches for the African National Congress. His efforts earned him the secretary general's position and a prison booking in Lusaka. While in prison, Kaunda formulated humanism, a concept that expresses faith in the common men and women as well as a belief in non-violence. Looking back today, this concept made him feel the pain others under the yoke of oppression felt.

He then left ANC to form the Zambian African National Congress that was driven underground by the British who arrested and brought him to Salisbury (Harare) Prison. When he left Salisbury Prison, he founded the United National Independent Party (UNIP) that joined hands with Dr Banda's Congress Party to fight the federation. In 1962, he became a legislative Council of Northern Rhodesia as a Minister of Local Government and Social Welfare in a UNIP/ANC coalition government. He assumed the presidency of the Republic of Zambia in 1964.

Of course, it's a fact that he lost the 1991 election to Chiluba because the Zambian economy was swapped and the nation was wallowing in poverty. Unlike Mobutu Sese Seko of Zaire and many other African leaders who drive their economies into the ground because of greed and insensitivity, Kaunda was a victim of many things. But before looking into the machinations formulated to effect his downfall, it would help a lot to list down what he did for Zambia.

When he took over, enrolment in schools and colleges rose from 3million to 7 million and infrastructure such as roads, clinics and colleges were built. He introduced the National Development Plans from 1964 to 1970 under which his reconstruction plans were carried out. But just like any other African nation, Zambia was a welfare nation. This state of affairs is usually a result of trying to cater for previously marginalised people. So in the early days of independence, Zambians enjoyed state subsidies on maize meal and other products. This, however, backfired when the copper prices fell such that by 1986, the economy could not hold.

The International Monetary Fund (IMF) had advised Zambia to devalue the kwacha, freeze wages and control public expenditure. The ripple effect of this was price hikes and massive shortages of commodities. By 1987, it was clear that Zambia was drowning and Dr Kaunda cut ties with both IMF and World Bank. What many people seem to forget is what caused the decline in Zambia's economy. Most attribute it to Kaunda's mismanagement yet there were various factors.

To begin with, when Ian Smith declared the Unilateral Declaration of Independence in 1965, he cut off the shortest route for the transportation of copper to South Africa from Zambia because Kaunda sheltered ZAPU and ZANU, organisations fighting Smith. This was costly for the country. With no help from the international community, Kaunda had to team up with Julius Nyerere and the Chinese in constructing the 1860 km Tanzania Zambia Railway (Tazara). A 1710km pipeline, the Tanzania, Zambia and Malawi (Tazama) that stretched from Dar es Salaam to Kapiri Mposhi was built. More hydroelectricity stations were built at the Kafue Gorge and Kariba's North Bank while industries were established to withstand the liberation struggle with farming systems improved to boost local food production.

In a 2001 report titled Zambia Against Apartheid compiled by and the Justice Centre for Theological Reflection (JCTR) estimates the cost of southern Africa's war on Zambia at US$19 billion. Of this figure, US$5,34 billion was incurred fighting apartheid alone. The report notes that 2010 data 'should be higher'. The report further says.

> Support for the liberation of Zimbabwe and others contributed to Zambia going into debt and through harsh IMF and World Bank debt conditions, staying in debt. And some forces that for gain supported racist regimes have come through other windows and are getting facilities and resources built by Zambia during the liberation. In April 1994, when apartheid South Africa changed and Nelson Mandela became president, Africa's liberation sights were reached. But for Zambia, there were no systematic international or local processes of healing from Southern Africa's war of liberation.

Although the fight against racism was a task for human dignity, the reports say, there has been no foreign material and economic support to help Zambia's rehabilitation. Thus various imbalances continue in society. Apart from the economic effects the wars caused on Zambia, the report says Zambia had to increase spending on defence and security because of 'bombings by racist regimes led to thousands of deaths of Zambians and freedom fighters. Many were maimed'.

Despite all these sacrifices, Dr Kaunda's legacy is not fully recognised, and it's saddening that when he was admitted in a Namibian hospital, the leaders he helped ascend to power were gathering in Windhoek discussing the future of liberation war movements. They also gathered in Luanda, Angola for the Southern African Development Community (SADC)'s chairmanship handover for an organisation he was the first chairman. If we go back again to the Mandela/ Kaunda parallel, one would ask: What is the difference between the two? Why has not the west been good to Dr Kaunda for bringing freedom to the region just like they are good to Mandela? Who is a better statesman – one who fights for others' freedom and one who does not condemn democracy's undemocratic ways?

If it's for peace, during his entire rule, Dr Kaunda never called for violence. It was his paramount desire to inculcate peace hence the peace that prevails among tribes in Zambia today. If it's fighting for HIV/Aids, Dr Kaunda has done much for this cause through his Kenneth Kaunda Children of Africa Foundation. Like Mandela, Dr Kaunda is respected in his country where he lives like an ordinary citizen. While the west can be justified in dumping Dr Kaunda in the dustbin of history, what about the region he helped free? It appears as if time and history are drowning Dr Kaunda's voice calling for togetherness and understanding among all the peoples of the region. With time, we won't hear his signature tune: Tiyende Pamodzi Ndi Mutima Umo!

- 14 November 2012 (Southern Times)

Nyerere's elusive dream: African unity

The late Tanzanian president Julius Nyerere was one of the founding fathers of the Organisation of African Unity, and he spent his entire life pushing for the attainment of this goal.

In his speech delivered in Zambia in 1966 when former president Kenneth Kaunda became the University of Zambia chancellor, Nyerere expressed his great concern about the failure by African leaders to foster unity and move the continent. In short, Nyerere spoke about how various African nationalisms conflicted with pan-Africanism.

He pointed out that while Africa had by then achieved much, the road ahead was still long and that he believed, '...there is a danger that we might now voluntarily surrender our greatest dream of all.' He explained:

> For it was as Africans that we dreamed of freedom, and we thought of it for Africa. Our real ambition was African freedom and African government. The fact that we fought are by area was merely a tactical necessity. We organised ourselves into the Convention People's Party, the Tanganyika African National Union, the United National Independence Party, and so on, simply

because each local colonial government had to be dealt with separately.

Nyerere asked whether 'Africa shall maintain this internal separation' if at all we are to proudly stand up and declare that 'I am an African.' He said:

It is not a reality now. For the truth is that there are now 36 different nationalities in free Africa, one for each of the 36 independent states—to say nothing of the still under colonial or alien domination. Each state is separate from the others: each is a sovereign entity. And this means that each state has a government which is responsible to the people of its area— and to them only; it must work for their particular well-being or invite chaos within its territory.

According to Nyerere, while pan-Africanism demands African consciousness and loyalty, the fact that pan-Africanists have to contend with developing their nations even by joining hands with erstwhile colonisers brings an element of conflict.

In one sense, of course, the development of part of Africa can only help Africa as a whole. The establishment of a University College in Dar es Salaam, and of a University in Lusaka, means that Africa has two other centres of higher education for its 250 million people. Every other hospital means more health facilities for Africa; every new road, railway or telephone line implies that Africa is pulled closer together. And who can doubt but that the railway from Zambia to Tanzania, which we are determined to build, will serve African unity, as well as being to the direct interest of our two countries? Unfortunately, however, that is not the whole story. Schools and universities are part of an educational system—a national educational system. They promote, and they must promote, a national outlook among the students. Lessons are given on the Government, the geography, and the history, of Tanzania, or of Zambia. Loyalty to the national constitution, to the elected leaders, to the symbols of nationhood—all these things are encouraged by every device, he further explained.

While all this was inevitable, Nyerere said, the colonial boundaries are a hindrance and make it impossible for those from other countries to access all these facilities.

Our present boundaries are - as has been said many times - the result of European decisions at the time of the Scramble for Africa. They are senseless; they cut across ethnic groups, often disregard natural physical divisions, and result in many different language groups being encompassed within a state. If the present states are not to disintegrate it is essential that deliberate steps be taken to foster a feeling of nationhood. Otherwise our present multitude of small countries—almost all of us too small to sustain a self-sufficient modern economy—could break up into even smaller units—perhaps based on tribalism. Then a further period of foreign domination would be inevitable. Our recent struggles would be wasted, he said.

While Africa has remained primarily divided politically, Nyerere also noted that economies had significantly contributed to the divide. He said that each African country has to fight for its survival without caring a hoot about 'development of Central Africa or East Africa'. This, Nyerere urged does not contribute to any meaningful growth but a 'reduction in unity'.

> All of the states of Africa need to attract capital from outside, and all of us wish to sell more of our goods to countries abroad. So we 36 small states each spend money to send our delegations to the wealthy countries, and our representatives to trade talks. Then each one of these national representatives is forced to prove why investment should be made in his country rather than in another and forced to offer some advantages to the wealthy country if it will buy his goods rather than those emanating from another part of Africa. And the result? Not only worse terms for each of us concerning aid or trade but also a kind of fear of each other - a suspicion that the neighbouring country will take advantage of any weakness we have for its benefit. And my point is that this neighbouring country will do that; it has little choice in the matter. However, much it may sympathise with our difficulty, only in rare cases will this sense of 'oneness' be able to transcend the hard necessities of its own economic need, he said.

Nyerere bemoaned the drift caused by such a scenario and urged for 'definite and deliberate counteracting steps' to be taken or risk dead nationalism in the long run. According to Nyerere, Africans have a willingness to unite against poverty because: 'They could not, and would not, agree to stagnation or regression while we pursue the goal of unity.' He repeated the fact that individualism entrenches differences inherited from the colonial period and develop new ones.

This is the dilemma of the Pan-Africanist in Africa now. For although national pride does not automatically preclude the development of pride in Africa, it is very easily twisted to have that effect and certainly it will be deliberately bolstered by those who are anxious to keep Africa weak by her division or those anxious to keep Africa divided because they would rather be important people in a small state than less important people in a bigger one, he stated.

Interestingly, Nyerere touched on the issue of how African countries are labelled and then divided into Chinese, Russian or French controlled spheres.

Kenyans and Zambians will be told - indeed are already being told - that Tanzania is communist and under Chinese control or that it is so weak that it is the unwilling and unwitting base for Chinese subversion. Tanzanians, on the other hand, are told that Kenya is under American control and Zambia hostile to it because of its policy on Rhodesia. And so on. Everything will be done and said which can sow suspicion and disunity between us until finally our people and our leaders say: 'Let us carry on alone, let us forget this mirage of unity and freedom for the whole of Africa', he said.

African unity, he said, is possible if the people are willing to face the dangers and overcome them because 'platitudes are not enough;

signatures to the Charter of the Organization of African Unity are not enough'.

Both these things help because they maintain the atmosphere and the institutions of unity. But they must be combined with a realisation that unity will be difficult to achieve, and challenging to maintain, and that it will demand sacrifices both from nations and from individuals. To talk of unity as though it would be a panacea of all ills is to walk naked into a den of hungry lions. In its early stages, unity brings difficulties—probably more than it disposes of. It is in the longer term, after 15 or 20 years, that its overwhelming benefits can begin to be felt, he explained.

- July 2015 (Southern Times)

Impoverishing a continent

The Zambian director of the anti-poverty group, Women for Change Emily Sikazwe, frustrated by the International Monetary Fund and the World Bank's policies in her country asked: 'What would they [the World Bank and the IMF] say if we took them to the World Court in The Hague and accused them of genocide?'

Sikazwe asked the question in 2007 years before the financial crises hit Greece, Portugal, Ireland and Spain. It was the time when most African countries under the IMF's Structural Adjustment Programs (SAPs) were reeling from shortages. Her concerns came after several analysts have, over the years, voiced their concerns with the way the IMF and the World Bank adopted destructive policies which left the continent in a far worse situation. While the affected in Europe have voiced their concern, the majority in Africa have been fed the IMF and World Bank's starvation diet silently.

Maybe the international writer on politics specialising in US policy towards the Third World, Asad Ismi, aptly summed up what the IMF and the World Bank do to Africa in his report titled *Impoverishing a Continent: The World Bank and IMF in Africa*. Robert Naiman and Neil Watkins of Centre for Economic and Policy Research (CEPR) in their 1999 paper, *A Survey of IMF Structural Adjustment in Africa: Growth, Social Spending and Debt Relief* say for about 20 years, the World Bank and the IMF have forced developing countries to create conditions that benefit Western corporations and governments.

These conditions are known as Structural Adjustment Programs (SAPs). SAPs require governments to cut public spending, (including eliminating subsidies for food, medical care and education); raise interest rates, thus reducing access to credit; privatise state enterprises; increase exports; and reduce barriers to trade and foreign investment such as tariffs and import duties. These measures are supposed to generate export-led growth that will attract foreign direct investment and can be used to reduce debt and poverty.

Dr Gloria Emeagwali, a professor of History and African Studies at Central Connecticut State University, New Britain, United States concurs with Naiman and Watkins in her study *Market Reform and Corporate Globalisation*. But Naiman and Watkins, Emeagwali adds that IMF policies cause forced currency devaluation which leads to a free fall in the value of domestic currencies and ultimately lower purchasing power and living standards. Also, IMF policies cause massive unemployment through retrenchment of workers and bring about high prices which trigger food riots and social unrest. The effects of privatisation are, among others, the de-industrialisation of economies and reduce local ownership of companies because they can't afford to buy into companies.

The removal of health subsidies has led to widespread increased mortality rate while that on education is responsible for massive school drop-outs and child labour. Most often, subsidies on schooling affect girl children because parents will opt to send boys to school. The long-term effect is an uneven and the feminisation of poverty, she writes. When the economy declines because of IMF policies, Emeagwali further notes, democratic governance is prejudiced, and it gives rise to ethnic politics as well as possible military dictatorships. Ironically, the IMF measures have led to increased debt for nations which saw a transfer of as much as 40% of the domestic budget to debt repayment to creditors or bankers of Euro-America. Once that percentage of a budget is reserved for debt repayment, a nation loses its sovereignty.

A three-year multi-country study released in April 2002 that included Zimbabwe, Ghana and Cote d'Ivoire done by the Structural Adjustment Participatory Review International Network (SAPRIN) in conjunction with World Bank, national governments and civil society say SAPs have been 'expanding poverty, inequality and insecurity around the world'. The report titled The Policy Roots of Economic Crisis and Poverty: A Multi-Country Participatory Assessment of Structural Adjustment says.

They have] torn at the heart of economies and the social fabric...increasing tensions among different social strata, fueling extremist movements and delegitimising democratic political systems. Their effects, particularly on the poor are so profound and pervasive that no amount of targeted social investments can begin to address the social crises that they have engendered.

SAPRIN further says IMF reforms impoverish and increase economic inequality,

First, trade and financial sector reforms have destroyed domestic manufacturing leading to massive unemployment of workers and small producers. Second, agricultural, trade and mining reforms have reduced the incomes of small farms and poor rural communities as well as their food security. Thirdly, labour market flexibilisation measures and privatisations have caused mass layoffs of workers and resulted in lower wages, less secure employment, fewer benefits and erosion of workers' rights and bargaining power.

Privatisation, the report also notes, of significant national assets and essential services has also allowed multinational corporations to remove resources and profits from countries as well as increase rates for water and electricity which has hit the poor the hardest. Besides, the cutting of health and education spending under SAPs and the introduction of user fees for these services, when combined with higher utility rates, has resulted in a severe increase in the number of poor as well as a deepening of poverty. In the process, the report says,

> Third World countries are forced to open their economies to Western penetration and increase exports of primary goods to wealthy nations. These steps amongst others have multiplied profits for Western multinational corporations while subjecting Third World countries to horrendous levels of poverty, unemployment, malnutrition, illiteracy and economic decline. The region worst affected has been Africa.

This, according to the report, should not come as a surprise because the US and IMF have become synonymous, 'Washington's predominance ensured that whatever their theoretical mandates might be, the World Bank and the IMF would become instruments of U.S. foreign policy. The role of both has been to fully integrate the Third World into the U.S.-dominated global capitalist system in the subordinate position of raw material supplier and open market. 'As such, these institutions complement the US' use of the Pentagon and the CIA to crush Third World governments aspiring to independent development.'

The report gives the example Chile's Salvador Allende in 1972 when President Richard Nixon and Henry Kissinger who was his National Security advisor then used IMF to destabilise the South American country. This action led to the bloody 1973 coup which murdered Allende and ushered in the military dictatorship of General Augusto Pinochet whose regime received $350.5 million, almost 13 times the $27.7 million the former received in three years. The height of the US influence was during the tenure of Robert McNamara at the financial institution from 1968 till 1981 when President Johnson worked to speed up the integration of Third World countries into the expanding US markets.

But by the 80s, most of the countries couldn't afford to pay back thereby giving Washington to use the IMF and the World Bank to subject Third World countries to SAPs. Apart from forcing currency devaluations and other measures, the US also got involved in labour laws, health care, environmental regulations, civil service requirements, energy policies and procurement.

The debt crisis gave the IMF room to be involved with governments, and as a writer and political commentator for the Toronto Star, Richard Gwyn note in his article *IMF Now Defacto Government for Millions* the IMF oversaw the lives of more than 1.4 billion people in 75 developing countries. This involvement has, in some cases, become destabilisation when the austerity measures force developing nations to reduce current accounts deficits by contracting money supply; demand strict anti-inflationary policy; privatise public enterprises; liberalise trade and dismantle foreign exchange controls and reduce the size of the public sector.

At the height of SAPs between 1980 and 93, the IMF subjected 70 developing countries to 566 stabilisation SAPs without any positive results and between 1984 and 1990, Third World countries doddering under SAPs paid more than US$178billion to western commercial banks. This, the report says, left developing countries reeling in poverty and destroyed health and educational infrastructure. Two prominent figures raised their voices against the IMF Fund in the late 80s and early 90s, were former World Bank director, Morris Miller and former UN Secretary-General, Javier Perez de Cuellar in 1991.

Filipino author and political analyst, Shea Cunningham and consultant Bill Rau in their report *IMF/World Bank: Devastation by Design, Covert Action* said:

Not since the conquistadors plundered Latin America has the world experienced such a flow in the direction we see today.

Ismi in *Plunder with a Human Face: The World Bank* that ran in the Z Magazine in 1998 claims that one of the most affected South American countries was Peru where about four million people were left in poverty when their wages were cut.

Consequently, there was a forced migration of impoverished peasants and urban unemployed into cocoa growing (for drug traffickers) as an alternative to starvation. In 1991, in exchange for US$100 million from the United States, Peru put in place the IMF structural adjustment clause opening its markets to US corn. As a result, by 1995, corn cultivation had fallen tenfold, and coca production had grown by 50 per cent. Under these conditions, corruption flourished; indeed almost an entire economy was criminalised. Increased cocoa production meant more cocaine trafficking which led to deepening official corruption in Peru as the amount of money in the hands of drug lords increased.

Raymond added on the Peru experience, 'From one day to the next, fuel prices increased 31 times- by 2,968%. The price of bread increased 12 times-by 1,150%. The prices of most basic food staples increased by six or seven times - 446% in a single month - yet wages had already been compressed by 80% in the period before the adoption of these measures in August 1990.'

Former South America Newsweek bureau chief and a California-based journalist David Schrieberg in *Dateline Latin America: The Growing Fury, Foreign Policy (1997)* describes Latin America as experiencing 'its worst period of social and economic deprivation in half a century'.

'By 1997, nearly half of the region's 460 million people had become poor - an increase of 60 million in 10 years. Populations, overall, were worse off than they were in 1980.' Even the United Nations Economic Commission for Latin America and the Caribbean (ECLAC) stated in 1996 that "the levels of [poverty] are still considerably higher than those observed in 1980 while income distribution seems to have worsened in virtually all cases".

As part of its new mandate, the IMF also had a low-intensity conflict (LIC) policy in the 80s pushed by the US targeting Grenada, Panama, Nicaragua, Angola, Panama, El Salvador and Guatemala as well as the Philippines. The LIC involved financing conflicts as a way of controlling the Third World. This was also meant to break and whip it into line a Third World that was demanding a new international economic order.

George H. W Bush also pursued this policy with the help of the IMF and the World Bank such that by 1993 Latin American government considered to be radical and revolutionary had been deposed. Nicaragua fell victim to this during Ronald Reagan's tenure when the Contras attacked the Sandinista government while the World Bank, under Thomas Clausen, a Reagan appointee pulled the plug on funding. Sub Saharan Africa too was caught up in the scheme of things, and as of 1980, 36 out of 47 countries were under SAPs.

In Africa IMF and World Bank policies slowed down growth; increased poverty levels; lowered income; caused low human development; increased debt burden; decreased health care and caused an increase in diseases; and affected education. American economist, columnist and co-director of the Centre for Economic and Policy Research (CEPR) in Washington Mark Weisbrot, Naiman, and Joyce Kim in their paper *The Emperor Has No Growth: Declining Economic Growth Rates in the Era of Globalization,* CEPR, November 27, 2000, said during 1960-1980, Sub Saharan Africa's GDP per capita grew by 36% but fell by 15% in the 1980-2000 period. 'These are enormous differences by any standard of comparison and represent the loss to an entire generation - of hundreds of millions of people - of any chance of improving its living standards,' they say.

The World Bank notes that in 1994 about 200 million people lived below the poverty line of US$ per day, but by 2003, the figure had increased by 75% to 350million.The bank further notes that per capita incomes for most Sub Saharan countries fell by 25% during the 1980s and for 18 countries these incomes were lower in 1999 than in 1975. United Nations, Development Programme (UNDP), Human Development Report, 2001; *UN, Economic Report on Africa 1999* says 80% of low human development countries - those with low income, low literacy, low life expectancy and high population growth rates - are in Africa.

Average life expectancy for Sub Saharan Africa is only 47 years (the lowest in the world), a drop of 15 years since 1980. Forty per cent of the population suffers from malnutrition that causes low birth weight among infants and stunts growth in children. In 2000, 30 per cent of children under five were underweight in Sub-Saharan Africa; thirty-seven per cent of such children were under height, the reports states.

Assistant director for policy analysis and communications at Africa Action, Ann-Louise Colgan in her position paper *Africa's Debt - Africa Action July 2001* argues that under SAPs, Africa's external debt has increased by more than 500% since 1980 to $333 billion today.

SAPs have transferred $229 billion in debt payments from Sub-Saharan Africa to the West since 1980. This is four times the region's 1980 debt. In the past decade alone, African countries have paid their debt three times over yet they are three times as indebted as ten years ago. Of Sub-Saharan Africa's 44 countries, 33 are designated heavily indebted developing countries by the World

Bank. Africa, the world's poorest region, pays the richest countries $15 billion every year in debt servicing. This is more than the continent gets in aid, new loans or investment.

According to the UNDP, if such payments were not made African would have 'saved 21 million people and given 90 million girls and women access to basic education by the year 2000'. The All-African Conference of Churches, a fellowship of churches and religious institutions described Africa's debt as 'a new form of slavery, as vicious as the slave trade' while Africa Action, a Washington DC-based advocacy group, says the US and rich countries are using Africa's debt as 'leverage to manipulate the continent's economic fate to serve their interest'. 'The US appears unwilling to support debt cancellation for Africa because the US gains a great deal from Africa's economic enslavement,' the organisation says.

Colgan in another paper *Hazardous to Health* and BBC's News Online environment correspondent Alex Kirby in *Water key to ending Africa's poverty 2002* say Africa spends four times more on debt interest payments than on health care.

Africa Action, *Africa's Right to Health Campaign: Background Links on Africa's Health* say, 'More than half of Africa's population is without safe drinking water, and two-thirds do not have access to adequate sanitation.' Oxfam Briefing Paper no. 19 notes that because of SAPs, '10 African governments spent more on debt repayments than on primary education and healthcare combined in 2002'.

This, the paper observes, leaves 40% of African children out of school, 'Between 1986 and 1996, per capita, education spending fell by 0.7% a year on average. The adult literacy rate in Sub-Saharan Africa is 60%, well below the developing country average of 73%. More than 140 million young Africans are illiterate.'

Emily Sikazwe, director of the Zambian anti-poverty group Women for Change, tells New Internationalist Magazine journalist Mark Lynas that SAPs cause poverty in 2007.

'And poverty has a woman's face,' she says.

- 14 November 2012 (Southern Times)

Figures don't lie – the state of our education

In the past 14 years, more than three million pupils sat for Ordinary Level in Zimbabwe, and of these only 470 000 passed. During this period, not more than 50 000 pupils passed Ordinary Level each year with more than five subjects, a trend which should not only worry Zimbabwe but make all those concerned sit back and discuss how to better the situation.

These frightening figures make it imperative to implement the recommendations made by the Nziramasanga Commission on Education in 1999. They also make Zimbabwe's much-celebrated education look like nothing much because there is no real success if 200 000 pupils sit for an exam and only 40 000 pass.

Last year's pass rate by the standards of the past 14 years is the highest. There was a 14,58% pass rate in 1998; 15,69% in 1999; 13,88 in 2000; 13,99% in 2001; 13,8% in 2002; 12,8% in 2003; 10,2% in 2004; 12% in 2005; 14,2% in 2006; 9,85% in 2007; 14,44% in 2008; 19% in 2009; 16,5% in 2010; 19,5% in 2011; 18,4% in 2012; and 20% in 2013. From 1998 to 2013 (minus 2004 and 2005) 3 161 633 pupils wrote their "O" level exams. Only 467 735 passed.

There were 244 083 "O" Level candidates in 1998, but only 35 593 passed. In 1999, 38 036 out of 242 329 candidates passed. Out of 264 056 who sat for the exams in 2000, only 36 659 passed. More than 272 125 wrote "O" Level exams in 2001 and out of these 38 077 passed. A year later, of the 274 772 took the exams, 37 804 passed. And only 35 606 out of 2003's 275 576 candidates passed. Only 31 247 of the 154 229 candidates for 2006 passed; 2007 had

25 673 out of 179 274; there were 20 632 passes from 142 840 examined in 2008; 16 853 managed five passes in 2009 when 87 201 sat for the exam; 2010 saw 37 871 passing out of 229 522 candidates; 45 887 of the 241 512 of the class of 2011 passed; of the 268 854 students tested in 2012, only 31 767 passed; while in 2013, 285 260 wrote the exams and 36 031 passed.

What happened to the 2 693 898 who failed the exams?

The Nziramasanga Commission had some of the solutions as to what should have been done with the 2 693 898 children who failed the academic exams.

The commission was appointed by President Robert Mugabe in 1998 to look into the problems in education and was chaired by senior research Fellow and associate professor Caiphas Nziramasanga.

One of the things the commission noted was that while education received the lion's share, 93% of the budget goes to salaries, leaving a mere 7% for operating costs. The commission also noted that the teaching standards had declined and failure rates were very high. It also took a swipe at poor administration and irrelevant curriculum.

Instead, the commission recommended vocationalised education, with rural schools concentrating on productive sectors in their respective areas. It also suggested that the teaching methods should be changed to focus on skills while reducing the focus on examinations. The saddest part is that Zanu PF and the government adopted the report last year in December during its 14th National People's Conference in Chinhoyi — 14 years later.

This means that during those 14 years, the problems found by the Nziramasanga Commission persisted unabated. It means that a whole generation — 2 693 898 — was lost — humanity broken.

Setting an impressive record, Zimbabwe's enrollment jumped from 819 586 in 1979 to 1 235 994 at independence and stood at 2 216 878 in 1985. By 1995, the figure had grown to 2 482 577 and to 2 509 153 in 1998. There was, however, a drop in 1999 from 2 509 153 to 2 488 939. Maybe this made Mugabe institute a commission of enquiry because by then 21% of primary school-going children were dropping out for lack of fees while 30% never made it to secondary school. There was nothing wrong with infrastructure then because the number of primary schools rose from 2 401 in 1979 to 4 234 in 1985, and to 4 723 in 1999. There were also no problems with qualified teachers then because by 1999 there were 59 973 trained teachers albeit a drop from the 66 502 of 1998. The number of teachers had steadily grown from the 28 455 in 1980 to 63 718 as of 1996. Secondary schools also experienced an increase in enrolment from 66 215 in 1979 to 148 690 in 1981. By 1995, there were 786 154 secondary pupils whose number went up to 806 126 by 1997. The number of secondary schools too increased from 177 in 1979 to 694 by 1981, and to 1 215 in 1985; 1 512 in 1990 and 1 531 in 1997.

This expansion was backed up by financial support, with education receiving the lion's share of the budget. Unfortunately, the budgetary allocations dwindled over the years, taking with them the excellent ordinary level pass rate which started to fluctuate. In 1980, it was, for example, 18,1% and five years later, it fell to 14,5%. By 1990, this had slid down to 14,3%. Although there was a slight increase in 1991 — to 15,3% — the allocation fell to 14% in 1992;

again in 1993 it went down to 12,9%; up a bit in 1994 to 13,6%, but slid to 12,8% in 1995 and then to 11,8% in 1996.

What went wrong?

Unstable political environment; a dead economy which drove away qualified teachers; disheartened and discouraged teachers who either spent much of their time on strike or just lazying around at schools; or even running side-businesses.

The European Commission also funded a report titled *A Rapid Assessment of Primary and Secondary Schools* in 2009 that was conducted by the National Advisory Board. This report concluded too that the quality of education declined because of a lack of teaching and sufficient learning materials. According to the study, between 2007 and 2008, 20 000 qualified teachers left the profession while 70 000 fled their posts between 2000 and 2008 because of political violence. A journal, European Social Sciences Research published in January 2013 by the Zimbabwe Open University (Zou) noted that out of a sample of 278 Zimbabwean schools, the teachers spoken to cited insufficient resources as one of the major problems.

The journal lists dilapidated buildings (50%); no piped water (67%); no electricity (92%); inadequate furniture (72%); lack of teaching material (94%) and inadequate textbook (100%). Some of the teachers cited political interference as an impediment to quality education, with polarisation taking centre stage.

Another report titled *Current Performance of the Education Sector in Zimbabwe: Key Policy Challenges Facing the Sector,* compiled by Louis Masuko and presented at a workshop on sectoral economic development, policy challenges and the way forward in 2003, says teachers made up the most significant number of emigrants. Masuko is from Economics and Technology Studies Institute of

Development at the University of Zimbabwe, and he submitted the paper during a workshop organised by the Zimbabwe National Chamber of Commerce and Friedrich Ebert Stiftung in Harare. In the paper, Masuko argues that the recorded number of teacher emigrants increased from 165 in 1998 to 210 in 1999. From 2000 the number rose to 352 before it reached 407 in 2001.

Masuko recommends policy intervention in the form of stabilising the macroeconomic environment; establishing a Graduate Investment Fund to promote self-employment; improving salaries and conditions of service for lecturers, teachers in general and for those in remote and rural areas; increase budgets for teaching materials; expanding the Basic Education Assistance Module programme to cater for school fees to the girl child; and making school calendar compatible with local economic activities.

- 20 February 2014 (Newsday)

Printed in the United States
By Bookmasters